T0208769

GUNNER

AN ENCHANTING TALE OF A RACEHORSE

VICTORIA HOWARD

authorHOUSE

AuthorHouse™
1663 Liberty Drive
Bloomington, IN 47403
www.authorhouse.com
Phone: 1 (800) 839-8640

The author is not liable for anything to be incorrect and hereby
disclaims any responsibility for them. Names have been changed for
protection of privacy. Although this is a true story and Gunner is
alive and well, certain parts have been embellished or fabricated.

Published by AuthorHouse 07/09/2020

ISBN: 978-1-7283-6489-6 (sc)
ISBN: 978-1-7283-6488-9 (e)

Library of Congress Control Number: 2020910925

Print information available on the last page.

Any people depicted in stock imagery provided by Getty Images are models,
and such images are being used for illustrative purposes only.
Certain stock imagery © Getty Images.

Scripture quotations marked KJV are from the Holy Bible,
King James Version (Authorized Version). First published
in 1611. Quoted from the KJV Classic Reference Bible,
Copyright © 1983 by The Zondervan Corporation.

Cover and all photos were taken by Amanda Diefenbach Photography

This book is printed on acid-free paper.

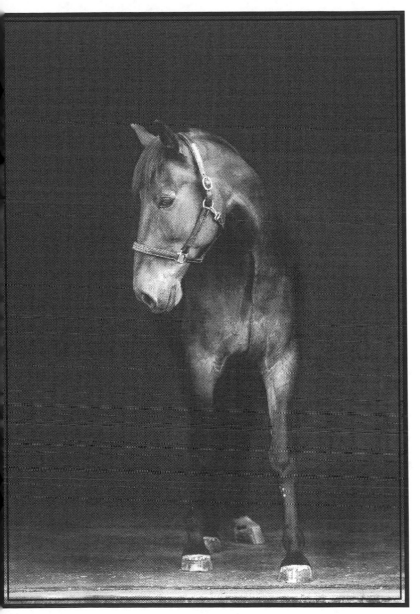

GUNNER

Dedication

To all my 4-legged children: Past, Present, and Future who have taught me the meaning of unconditional love. Until We Meet Again!

And to Nadine, Max, and Vivian Grace

Revelations 21: 4 "And God shall wipe always all tears from their eyes; and there shall be no more death, neither sorrow, nor crying, neither shall there be any more pain: for the former things are passed away."

Acknowledgments

*A VERY SPECIAL THANKS TO THE
STANDARDBRED RETIREMENT
FUND, CRAWFORD RETIREMENT,
PURPLE HAZE Standardbred Adoption
PROGRAM, and THE ONTARIO
STANDARDBRED ADOPTION AGENCY.*

*A portion of proceeds will go to the Equine Retirement Fund

Contents

Dedication   vii
Acknowledgments   ix
God Once Said   xv
Introduction   xvii
Preface   xix

PART ONE

Chapter 1	A Star Is Born	1
Chapter 2	My First Home	11
Chapter 3	No Longer A Stallion	21
Chapter 4	My Second Home	27
Chapter 5	A New Career	33
Chapter 6	The Life Of A Racehorse	45
Chapter 7	My First Race	53
Chapter 8	Understanding A Horse	67
Chapter 9	My Racing Career	73
Chapter 10	An Unwanted Horse	81

PART TWO

Chapter 11   My Third Home   87
Chapter 12   A New Type Of Life   93
Chapter 13   Home #4   99
Chapter 14   Becoming A Plow Horse   103
Chapter 15   The Killpen   107

PART THREE

Chapter 16   Sold!   113
Chapter 17   An Angel In Blue Jeans   121
Chapter 18   Free At Last   125
Chapter 19   My Forever Home   131
Chapter 20   My New Friends   137
Chapter 21   TLC–The Best Medicine   145
Chapter 22   A New Me   151
Chapter 23   Time For Work   157
Chapter 24   Becoming A Riding Horse   161
Chapter 25   Remount School   165
Chapter 26   Graduation Day   173

PART FOUR

Chapter 27   My New Career   181
Chapter 28   Scare Tactics   187
Chapter 29   Letting My Hair (Mane) Down   193
Chapter 30   Long Island   199
Chapter 31   My First Parade   205
Chapter 32   Independence Day   211
Chapter 33   Community Day   217
Chapter 34   A Close Call   223

Chapter 35	An American Hero	229
Chapter 36	The County Fair	235
Chapter 37	An Unexpected Injury	241
Chapter 38	Dreams Can Come True	247
Chapter 39	The End Of A Beautiful Story	255

Epilogue	259
About the Author	261
Rainbow Bridge	263
Other Equine Books Written by Victoria M. Howard	265

God Once Said

"I NEED SOMEONE STRONG ENOUGH TO PULL A CART, BUT GENTLE ENOUGH TO LOVE A CHILD, SMART ENOUGH TO PROTECT HIS MASTER AND PASSIONATE ENOUGH TO LOVE HIS FAMILY AND SOMEONE WITH SO MUCH LOVE THEY CAN LIFT THE SPIRITS OF A BROKEN HEART"

SO HE CREATED THE HORSE

Introduction

Fairytales! We all love fairytales because there's a piece of us, a sliver of innocence left from our youth that lay dormant which suddenly surfaces when revealed by a printed page or silver screen.

It's hidden in our inner self–the part that still believes in magical tales.

Looking at fairy tales through the lens of science reveals that some stories aren't as far-fetched as they appear to be. This is where the wonders of pure imagination kicks in.

Many stories focus on animals that are the eternal underdogs, for who didn't love reading about Bambi, Lassie, and Black Beauty? They are essentially fairy tales, but hauntingly told with a modicum of truth and reality.

The ingenious Mr. Walt Disney did it best as his characters came to life via animation–bringing fantasy and imagination to reality by utilizing the tried and tested 'feel good' philosophy that 'Dreams Can Come True.'

That is, after some trials and tribulations of course.

Although the story of **Gunner** is factual, parts have been exaggerated in adherence to pure storytelling.

In true Disney-like inspiration **Gunner** is the basic 'Rags to Riches' saga about an ordinary racehorse that overcomes incredible adversity to emerge as the equine legend he is today.

Make no mistake, Gunner, as you will discover, is the Steven Hawking, Emily Davison, and Joan of Arc of the equine world. He is the Rambo that withstood and conquered inhumane situations to rise as the ultimate paragon for horses.

After reading his story, formulate your own conclusion. Can horses really communicate with one another? Do they connect with and even reflect human emotions? Is there an elusive Rainbow Bridge between Heaven and Earth where departed pets idyllically await their owners' crossing?

Personally, I think even Mr. Disney would have enjoyed the story of **Gunner!**

Read this book with an open mind and believe 'Anything Is Possible' and 'Dreams Can Come True.'

Victoria

Preface

One day a woman named Mary Elena Moran called wanting to know if I'd be interested in writing a book about her horse. She told an extraordinary tale, but didn't know how to put it on paper. Emotions stirred as I heard the gruesome life her horse endured.

Initially, somber emotions turned to rage as how anyone could treat an animal, then rage became joy that someone had the compassion and humanitarianism to rescue and provide sanctuary to this incredible horse.

That horse is Gunner, but his racehorse name is Gun-It. Today, Gunner is an eighteen-year-old equine that survived several wars. Although his physicality was dilapidated, his spirit could not be broken!

Gunner's story is a conglomeration of Black Beauty, Sea Biscuit, and perhaps Kelso, for he is the underdog who beat the odds to emerge a hero.

The story of **Gunner** is for anyone who appreciates one of God's most beautiful creations--the HORSE. It is a true-life adventure: although several parts have been slightly exaggerated to enhance the literary authenticity.

It details Gunner's life from a colt, to an innocuous racehorse, to buggy horse, to kill pen to the Super horse he is today.

As a writer I tend to write from a child's perspective for there's a part of me that never grew up. I've always seen things through rose-colored glasses–barriers that once seemed impenetrable transformed into exciting opportunities.

My mother always said I lived in a fairy-tale-world. Maybe I did and still do, for the world today is bombarded with scandals, disease and riots: so I tend to see it in a way that makes sense to me.

We all need to hear and read something inspirational that gives us hope to an ambiguous future. For that reason I wrote this story narrated in the first person as an autobiographical memoir told by Gunner himself—"*Straight From the Horses Mouth!*"

It's a magical tale that entertains, educates, and elevates while revealing the appalling situation of many horses and what we can do to eradicate it.

Revelation 19:11 Then I saw heaven opened and behold, a white horse! The one sitting on it is called Faithful and True, and in righteousness he judges and makes war.

I AM HIS EYES
HE IS MY WINGS
I AM HIS VOICE
HE IS MY SPIRIT

PART ONE

Chapter One

A STAR IS BORN

No Heaven Can Heaven Be, If My Horse Isn't There To Welcome Me

Told by Gunner

As I stand outside a New York kill pen, I watch trailers arrive unloading dozens of rejected horses. It's déjà vu of the unpleasant memory when I was here on Horse Death Row. But thankfully, a lot has happened since then.

Today, I am the advocate and spokes-horse for all equines sentenced to death because they can no longer race, or are wanted or needed. I hope my story helps put an end to this abominable situation that exists worldwide.

My life has come to a full circle, and I am thankful to God for that.

You may pick this up and say, "*Oh, it's just another horse book!*" Well my friend, I guarantee that is not the case! You see just because I'm a horse doesn't mean I'm some stupid nag with no feelings or a story worth telling.

If something newsworthy occurs in the human world, it makes the 5 o'clock news: horrific and depressing things such as murder, rape, riots and the corona virus.

But when one of my own, not necessarily a horse, but any animal is tortured, ends up in a kill pen, or tossed aside like a piece of old trash, it's considered inconsequential.

I'm not saying I'm special or better than other horses, but I endured many years of abuse to rise and stand on all four legs to tell you my story. So, if you're an emotional chap that cries when hearing about the mistreatment of an animal, you better get a box of tissues because you're going to need it.

They say everyone and everything has a purpose in life–well, I believe this is mine. My name is Gunner and this is my story.

Present Day

Today is January 1, 2020. It's a brand new year and I'm a year older. You see, all racehorses celebrate their birthday on the first of January, no matter what month and day they were actually born. I'm 18-years-old in horse years, which makes me approximately 55 in human years (give or take a month).

Ha! In a few more years I'll be old enough to collect Social Security, but unfortunately there is no economic assistance or pension available for us four-legged creatures.

Most of my family and friends are either dead or sent places I don't want to think about. As I reminisce the way my life was, and what it's like today, I thank God (*Yes–we have the same God*) for although I've been through horrific times, today I live on a farm with a family that truly loves and cares for me.

My friends call me Gunner, so now that you're my friend you can too. If you think the name Gunner is funny, infinitely it's better than 'Gun-It' that's typed on my registration papers.

A registration paper is basically an equine birth certificate disclosing name, sex, the day the horse is born, and their immediate parentage.

My dams (mother) name is Run-N-Gun and my sire (father) is Cole Muffler.

Poor Mama! Boy, did I make her scream on March 12, 2002 (sorry Mom) when I made my debut into this crazy world, for I was a rather large colt.

I was born in Big Rock, Illinois, and what you call a Standardbred horse: A breed known for either pacing or trotting. In my case, I was born to pace, like both my parents.

Standardbreds, aka/ harness horses, can compete until they're 14 years old, but only a handful race to that age for the wear, tear, and pounding on the racetrack take its' toll on our delicate, fragile legs.

When a racehorse's career is over the fortunate ones may be adopted as riding horses, show horses, therapy horses, jumpers, or family pets. Unfortunately, way too many end up in horse hell (kill pens) like I did!

I'm not your "normal" horse for:

1) I believe in God
2) I love country music
3) Although I'm a gelding, I'm what you'd call a "ladies man"
4) I've carried the flag honoring the veterans
5) I have a day named after me
6) I was given the key to the city by the Mayor

Before I begin, I'll tell you a little about my lineage. My dad Cole Muffler was a decent pacing horse that amassed $682,380 during his racing career. (Remember, this was in the early 90's when that went a lot further than it would today.)

I'm what you'd call 'royally bred' on my father's side for dad's by Cole Muffler who is by Tyler B and my great-grandfather is Most Happy Fella and my great-great grandfather is the remarkable breed changer Meadow Skipper!

On my mother's side, my grandmother is Siren Almahurst who produced a near champion named Nuclear Siren. (He was very well known in that era)

As for me, I wasn't great on the track, but I wasn't a nonentity. I managed to earn some money for my owners, which helped pay my keep and took a decent race record for that time frame.

At one time it looked like I was going to be an ATM machine; (moneymaker) that is, until my physical soundness deteriorated.

As far as bodily appearance: I'm a very large bay with a 'pretty head' that stands 17 ½ hands—which is considered tall for a standardbred.

Unfortunately, when I was born I emerged with two crooked front legs, which caused me to toe in.

Traditionally, a horse, especially a pacer that toes in can brush his knees while in motion and that can be mighty painful. And a horse with crooked legs places uneven pressure on his joints. This encumbrance predisposes them to inflammation and soft tissue damage as well as deterioration of the cartilage.

Not a good thing! So from the very start, I had a huge strike against me.

Early on I was gelded so there was zero chance of me becoming a stallion when my racing days ended. That would have been nice for studs get paid big bucks for doing what they do best--courting mares!

With my laid back disposition I would have made a nice riding horse or a little girl's pet, but sadly that didn't happen.

My final race took place on May 15, 2009. During five years competing I earned almost $26,000, ending my career with 104 starts: 6 wins, 9 seconds and 15 thirds.

Not great, but nothing to sneeze at.

Periodically, people called Amish came to the barn looking to purchase injured horses that could no longer race. They dressed different than most people. The women wore their hair tucked under bonnets and donned long dresses. The men wore trousers with suspenders and most had bushy beards.

I remember the time my ex-girlfriend, Cleo, was sold to the Amish. Every time I think about her I get teary eyed for she was my first love! Cleo was a big black trotting mare with the sexiest whinny.

As I said, I was gelded so I couldn't impregnate her, thus we were turned out together. We'd run and chase one another--then we would stand side-by-side eating grass.

Cleo knew when I wasn't feeling well or having a bad day. She would trot over and nuzzle my neck, assuring me all was well, and when she did, goose bumps ran down my legs.

Being a gelding meant I could no longer perform and produce foals, but the vet must have missed a piece for I still experienced fuzzy sensations—especially around Cleo. But knowing I was totally harmless she let me tease her. Typical woman!

Then it happened! One day Cleo was in a race accident and tore her suspensory. The vet determined the injury was severe and she would never race again.

The next morning I woke to find those bearded men in the barn. When they took Cleo out of her stall they were impressed for she was a big black mare and everyone knows Amish love black trotting mares.

A deal was made and as Cleo walked on the truck she bellowed, *"Please don't let them take me away, Gunner. I don't want to go."*

I thought, *"Oh no, they're taking someone I love away again, just like when they took my mother."*

My heart broke. I thrashed and banged against the stall trying to break out, but it was fruitless. I heard her fading whinny as the trailer drove out of sight. Little did I know one day I would be reunited with my Cleo.

Chapter Two

MY FIRST HOME

To See The Winds Power, The Rain's Cleansing And The Sun's Radiant Life, One Need Only To Look At The Horse

My very first recollection was that of a large meadow with a frozen lake of murky water. Several trees lined the perimeter, but since it was mid-winter they were barren. Records were broken due to the blistery temperatures Illinois got. Nighttime was downright frigid, but I was never cold for my mother kept me warm.

Mama had a thick winter coat that I nestled into and when it snowed she stood over me so I would stay dry.

A mother is one of God's greatest creations for He made her out of clouds, angel hair, and everything that's nice in the world. He took the fragrance of a flower, the majesty of a tree, the gentleness of morning dew, and the calm of a quiet sea.

She is the beauty of a twilight hour, the soul of a starry night, the laughter of the rippling brook, and the grace of a bird in flight. Then God fashioned from all these things a creation like no other and when His masterpiece was through He called it 'Mother.'

I loved my mother from the first time I saw her. I remember lying on the ground and getting wet kisses all over my body. When I opened my eyes, there was this beautiful big horse licking my face. It took me several attempts to get up, but when I did she guided me to a place under her belly.

I'll never forget that first drink of milk! Once I started, I couldn't quit! And although she was quite tired and sore from giving birth, mother let me drink as long as I wanted!

I was blessed for one of the other colts on the farm lost his mother at childbirth and had to nurse from what they call a 'surrogate' mare. I couldn't imagine being with anyone but my mother.

For the first few months I lived strictly upon mothers' milk, but even if I could eat grass there was none to be found.

During the day I ran alongside mom, never wanting to be far away. I guess you could call me a "momma's boy."

Five other colts and their dams were also in the field and across the creek were the fillies.

The colts loved to play, but I'd rather be with mom then them. Whenever one got too close she would shoo them away, for she was very protective of her first born.

Bill and Karen Smith were the proprietors of BK Stables. They raised standardbred racehorses and sold most as yearlings to offset the costs of the farm.

I kept hearing the word standardbred and wasn't sure what it meant, but would soon find out.

It's similar to a person's heritage. When you come from an Italian family you're Italian and when your parents are Irish, you are too. So in the horse world if your parents are standardbreds you're a standardbred, and if your parents are thoroughbreds than you're a thoroughbred.

Unlike thoroughbreds whose jockeys ride on their backs, the driver of a standardbred sits on a funny looking cart attached to the horse called a sulky.

———

Living at BK Stables was paradise for we never went without grain, were fed the best alfalfa hay, and bathed when we got dirty from playing in mud puddles. The best memories of my young life were at BK Stables and if I could have stopped time I would have.

Mother was known as "Queenie," basically because she ruled the other horses as the alpha mare.

Mom was Bill's favorite. He took time to brush and groom her each morning and she returned his kindness by nuzzling him and occasionally let Bill sit beside her in the grass. One time she even put her head on his lap!

He would stroke her and say, *"Good morning beautiful Queenie, and how is your big boy today?"*

I have to admit I got a little jealous, for that was MY mom and I should be the only one who got to lie beside her!

———

One day Karen asked Bill, *"It's time to name the colts. What do you want to call Queenie's?*

After a few minutes he answered, *"Let's name him Gun-It—but we'll call him Gunner."*

"I like that—he looks like a Gunner!" she laughed.

I thought to myself, "Gunner? That's a funny name. What's a Gunner supposed to look like?"

———

The months flew by and winter turned to spring. The hot sun peeked through the clouds melting the snow. Blades of grass sprouted through the ground and robins sang melodic songs while perched high in cherry blossom trees.

We were now weanlings and old enough to start eating grain so they fed us in rubber buckets placed alongside our mothers.

The tubs were far away from each other, for every now and then a mare would try to steal another's feed and a fight would start.

It could get downright ugly watching two mares kicking and striking! When that happened Bill put one in the barn so she could eat in peace.

I think it was about this time when I began playing with the other colts, for I got tired of watching them have all the fun. We ran up and down the rolling hills chasing one another, galloping as fast as our little legs would take us. I usually reached the top first, for even as a youngster I had quick, wicked speed.

Bill commented, *"Queenie's boy is really fast. I think he's going to make a good racehorse. Maybe we'll keep him."*

"I'd like that. There's something about him that's special," Karen said.

———

They say "boys will be boys," and I guess that's true for both humans and animals. Now and then a colt would bite or kick another and mother would intervene before anyone got seriously hurt.

One day a colt named Joey trotted over and began biting me. First he bit gently, then harder. I tried to ignore him, but the brat wouldn't stop. Mom saw what was happening, stood between us, and gave Joey a nasty look. He galloped off to bother another weanling for he was the bully of our group!

After mom saw I was okay she said, "*Son, in your life you will come across many types of horses. Some will be kind, while others will be mean like Joey. You were born to race like your dad and I, and although it can be an exciting life it can also be very dangerous.*

I hope you grow up to be kind and loving and never learn bad ways.

When you race, make sure to give it your all. You may not be as fast as other horses, but that doesn't matter as long as you do your best.

And always remain humble and thankful for what you have, and never envy others. And the same holds for humans. Not all people will be kind and caring like Bill and Karen, for there are many humans who are heartless and cold. I pray you will never have such owners."

Those words stuck with me for the rest of my life. Mom was a wise horse the others liked and respected. Although I never met my father, she said he was a handsome stallion and very good racehorse. I wanted to be just like dad when I grew up!

Although I had begun eating grain, I still occasionally nursed. That was my favorite time for the bonding process is priceless. Like a human mother and her baby: the role of breastfeeding is the best way to strengthen the bond by providing comfort of skin-to skin contact.

My baby teeth came in and were sharp. One time while nursing I inadvertently bit mom's nipple and drew blood. She swatted me with her tail, let out a blood-curdling squeal, and punished me by not allowing me to nurse until I promised to be gentler.

I was six-months-old when I experienced my first heartbreak–the first of many to come. All the horses were grazing when a truck and trailer pulled up and parked along the fence.

As several men approached the paddock gate the broodmares took off running. Like a mothers' intuition knowing something's wrong, the mares warned their colts.

"Run. Run as fast as you can," they told their boys.

My mom, the smartest of the bunch hid behind a huge oak tree.

One of the men put a lead on Joey's mother, Bessy, and led her out of the field and onto the trailer. I couldn't believe Joey was oblivious to the whole situation for he didn't seem to mind his mother leaving and continued stuffing his belly.

Three of the remaining four mares loaded on the trailer, leaving only my mother. Initially I thought she had outsmarted them, but then a man slid a lead over her nose and tugged on it.

Her maternal instincts kicked in. She planted her hooves and wouldn't budge, trying to protect me. Although the man was quite large, he was no match for my 1,200-pound mother.

When she wouldn't go with him, he got angry and hit her with the chain. She let out a screech and spun to kick him. I was shocked for I had never seen her act like that before.

She fired, missing the man's leg. He got really mad and smacked her harder!

Bill saw what happened and yelled, "*Don't you ever hit one of my horses. Now give me that damn lead and get the hell out of here.*"

The man mumbled something under his breath as he walked away. I thought, "Good ole' Bill saved the day–now maybe mom and I won't have to leave."

"*I'm sorry Queenie. Nobody will ever hit you again. You're probably wondering what's going on here. Your son is growing into a young man, and it's time we take him away. You and the other mares are going to live at my cousin's farm several miles from here. He's a kind man and will take care of you while we wean your boys. I promise to visit you every day until you return.*

And we have to get you ready to re-breed. You're such a good mother. Maybe your next foal will be a filly. I hope if it's a girl she's as pretty as you," Bill said.

19

"What? Wait a minute! I'm her baby and always will be. She doesn't need any other babies. Mom—tell Bill you don't want any other kids!"

But they were already on the other side of the fence. As she walked on the trailer I screamed, "MAMA! Please don't leave me. Come baaaaaaack!" as I ran the fence.

"Don't worry son, you will be fine. You were born for a reason and I know one day you're going to be famous. The good Lord has something very special planned just for you. I'll never ever forget you and will always love you," she whinnied as they drove off the farm.

Chapter Three

NO LONGER A STALLION

I Have Seen Things So Beautiful They Have Brought Tears To My Eyes–Yet None Of Them Can Match The Gracefulness And Beauty Of A Horse Running Free

It was another dreary day on the farm. Leaves changed colors and fell from the trees. Evenings were so cold Bill covered Running Boy and me in winter blankets. We were the only two yearlings left of the six born that year.

One by one my friends left for their new homes. First was Joey, destined for a Pennsylvania racetrack. Next were the two fillies, Su Mac Sara and Precious Girl, going to an Ohio trainer; and last to go were Markie and Petie, off to Delaware.

It was sad to see the fillies leave. Although I never got to know them, I'd see their pretty faces when they came to the main barn to get shod.

Boy, were they hot! Su Mac was a blue roan with a silver mane and tail, and Precious Girl was a dappled chestnut.

I was by far the tallest of the group. They said I was exceptionally handsome and resembled my mother. I vaguely remembered her for the broodmares never did return to BK Farm.

Bill decided to keep Running Boy and me for racing purposes and planned on sending us to his trainer Marvin at Sportsman's Park Racetrack in Chicago. It was this time that my testosterone levels soared, so Dr. Wes was called 'to settle me down.'

Ever since Bill caught me trying to mount Running Boy he kept us in separate fields. It was no fun being alone and that's when I really missed mom and wondered where and how she was.

Dr. Wes the farm veterinarian helped deliver and cared for me since I was born, so I didn't mind him poking me here and there. I knew he wouldn't hurt me and trusted him. That is, until that day!

One morning Doc came into my stall and stuck me in the neck with something sharp. The room was spinning as I fell to the ground. It felt like I was asleep, but I wasn't for I could hear him talking.

He scrubbed my private area with warm sudsy water and although it didn't hurt, it felt strange. Then that prickly thing happened again, but this time down there. I'm not sure how long I was out, but when I tried to get up my legs were wobbly.

Bill and Karen were there, waiting for me to awake. *"Well Gunner, I don't think you'll be wanting to mount horses anymore,"* he laughed.

I remained in my stall that entire week. Although I was sore, they said I healed great. When I was ready Marvin turned me out in the paddock. I looked for Running Boy, but didn't see him.

I overheard a groom say my friend had undergone the same operation as me, but complications arose and Running Boy crossed over the Rainbow Bridge.

I thought, "A Rainbow Bridge! That sounds like something fun. I wonder where it is? Maybe I could find it and go visit him someday."

This was the first of many times I would hear about this colorful magical bridge.

———————

Being the only yearling got quite lonely for horses are pack animals and would rather be with another than alone. I was depressed and stood in the corner with my head hung down. Accordingly, shortly after, Bill provided me with a Shetland pony named Molly who became my companion.

Chapter Four

MY SECOND HOME

All Horses Deserve, At Least Once In Their Lives, To Be Loved By A Little Girl

It was November when I left Bill and Karen: the first parents I had and the BEST!

They spent the entire evening in chairs outside my stall, just watching me. Karen was crying as Bill comforted her.

Bill said it was like sending their child off to college: explaining it was only temporary and most likely I would return.

Being good parents they were sad to see their '4-legged kid' leave, but assured me I was in good hands. And of course Molly would be coming, so I wouldn't be alone in a strange new place.

That morning Karen prepared me for my new journey. I had grown quite tall and in order to reach my back she had to stand on a small ladder. She commented 'if I had one mean bone in my body I would be dangerous,' but since I was sweet and mellow she nicknamed me, "The Gentle Giant."

When it came time for goodbye I couldn't do it and buried my nose in Karen's shoulder. She threw her arms around my neck and kissed me before running into the house.

"Don't mind Karen, big boy. She loves you so much and doesn't want you to leave. I don't either, but you have to go into the world and do what you were born to do–race. You'll be back, so until we meet again, be safe and show

them what you can do," he said as a tear ran down his cheek.

Marvin, the man who came to fetch Molly and Me was to be my trainer. When he saw me his mouth opened.

*"Holy moly, Bill, when you said the colt was big, I never imagined he was **this** big! I've **never ever** had a yearling this size. In fact, I've had very few racehorses this tall! He has to be 17 hands!"*

After Molly and I were loaded on the trailer, it seemed like we drove for days, although it was a mere six-hour drive to Sportsman's Park. I'm really not one for trailer rides for my head touches the roof and I'm a bit claustrophobic.

When the truck stopped there was snow on the ground. Marvin was careful to walk me–avoiding the ice patches for it wouldn't have been pretty seeing me fall.

Inside the barn, other horses whinnied welcoming us.

A pretty lady came over. *"This cannot be a yearling. I hope he's easy to work with, for if not, you better find another groom. I don't want to get hurt. You know how tricky it can be to work with a yearling. You have to watch them every minute."*

"I'll be handling him for the first week or two until we see what he's like. Don't worry, Cathy, I wouldn't give you a bad actor," Marvin assured her.

As I walked into what would be my home for the next five years, Molly followed close behind.

The stalls were much larger than Bills, and I was thankful for that.

My stall was clean with layers of straw that covered my ankles. In the top corner was a mounted rack full of fresh alfalfa, and on the ground was timothy for Molly.

The mare next door stretched her neck–her nose barely reaching my stall.

"Welcome, stranger. My name is Pretty Woman and as you can see I am called that for a good reason," she said batting her long lashes.

"I think she's flirting with you, Gunner," Molly laughed.

"Hello. My name is Gunner and yes, you are quite a pretty woman," I snorted.

I was always polite to others, especially the opposite sex. You see humans are not the only ones who communicate with each other.

Communication is taking place all the time among horses and unlike people they rarely communicate through vocal repertoire for they use body language and facial expressions.

Contrary to what you may believe, horses are highly intelligent and social, so it is understandable we communicate our feelings. We convey what we want by squeals, snorts, blows, and neighs. You may not know what we are saying, but we do!

To better educate you on how important smell is to animals, I will explain. Horses have a much better sense of smell than humans. The reason our head is so long is because we have a large nasal cavity that allows our nostrils to flare as we breathe a scent we're interested in.

Horses have a Vomeronasal Organ or Jacobson's Organ, which senses pheromones of the opposite sex–like when a stud sees a pretty mare.

Many times we'll lift our head and peel back our lips when we inhale a scent we like or don't. It looks like we're smiling–and guess what, we really are. You'll also see a horse curl their upper lip after getting a dose of medicine, which is our way of telling you we're not pleased with the taste!

When horses first meet they often touch noses or snort softly before exchanging squeals. God gave us this ability as a safety caution so we can smell areas that have been inhabited by bears or other predatory animals in the wild. This is a primal sense that kept our ancestors safe when they were in danger of becoming a meal.

Marvin introduced me to each horse by walking me up to their stall and smell each other. They were all nice, except one small gelding named Napoleon.

I soon discovered why he was given that name. He was a slight bay with an inferiority complex that bullied others to compensate his size.

Chapter Five

A NEW CAREER

A Large And Liquid Eye...The Swirl Of Dust Around Pounding Hooves.... These Then Are The Images That Moves Us

The first few days at my new house went smoothly. Each morning Marvin turned Molly and me out in a small paddock. It's good to get out of a 12 x 12 stall to run and play, for horses get tired of being cooped up. I mean--would you like to be confined to one tiny room? You would get stir crazy and want out. Well, so do we!

In a field we can roll and really stretch our legs. This is also how we scratch our backs from an itch or insect bite, and rolling also relieves tight muscles or stress.

Sometimes when we roll in a stall we get 'cast'– that's when we lie too close to the wall and can't get back on our feet. It can be dangerous for some horses panic, thrash, and get injured.

It was here I first heard and fell in love with country music. Marvin always had a radio on playing country songs. My favorite singers are Keith Urban, Travis Tritt, Billy Currington, and Gretchen Wilson. When I hear the music I move back and forth, which is my way of dancing.

When Marvin first saw me swaying back and forth he called the vet thinking something was wrong.

"Hey Doc. I'm afraid Gunner may have the wobbles or EPM. Every once in awhile his legs shakes and he sways back and forth!"

After numerous tests were done and all came back negative they walked me out of the stall to diagnose. The radio was playing one of my favorite songs and I began swaying in crossties. When Doc saw me he laughed and scratched his head.

"Well I'll be damned!" he said.

"I know this sounds bizarre, but I think Gunner is dancing."

"WHAT! Horses don't dance Doc," Marvin said.

After watching me every day and seeing I only did that when music was playing, he never questioned it again.

In fact, he really got a kick out of watching me dance, as did the other horses in the barn.

One day when I was grooving Pretty Woman nickered, *"Hey Gunner. You have some smooth, fancy moves."*

I want to think I'm a hopeless romantic. I dedicate a song to whoever my girlfriend is at the time and it's not hard to figure out which song was for my new love. It was Roy Orbison's 'Pretty Woman,' of course!

When she walked out of the stall, I sang to her.

"Pretty woman, won't you pardon me? Pretty woman, I couldn't help but see, Pretty Woman. Then you look lovely as can be. Are you lonely just like me?"

I know she liked it for she would smile and bat her eyes.

The first time I heard Billy Currington sing his new hit, I told Molly *"That's my theme song!"*

"What are you talking about?" she asked. *"What song?"*

"You know, the one that goes–'God is great, beer is good and people are crazy."

Yep—that's my song! God IS great—beer is mighty good and people are definitely crazy!

———

All the horses accepted me into their family--but unfortunately, not Molly. They would squeal and pin their ears at her--especially Napoleon!

Once he lunged at her as she passed his stall. Marvin said Napolean liked to bully Molly because she was more his size. The other horses thought it was funny, but I didn't.

"You're a funny looking thing," a mare said to Molly.

I could tell my little friend was hurt for she cowered in the corner.

"Don't mind her. She's just jealous, because you're so damn cute," Pretty Woman said.

That was my girl! She always knew the right thing to say!

———

On the third day Marvin walked me to the back of the barn where it was very noisy. As I entered a room, I smelled fire. I knew what fire was because Bill and Karen used to cook hot dogs, marshmallows, and smores by a campfire on the farm.

Sometimes Karen would sneak me a smore. I can still remember the taste of that gooey cookie!

One thing I love to do is eat. Occasionally, Marvin brought donuts, pizza, bananas, coconuts and beer to the barn. He said beer is actually good for horses because it helps our coats shine. It's made from yeast, which provides vitamin B-complex--and vitamin B complex provides horses with a nutritional component that helps them recover from stress.

He said horses wouldn't get fat or drunk from beer and most love the taste. In fact, at many tracks you can find beer in the barn for it also revitalizes and stimulates appetites in picky eaters! (Plus the trainers like to indulge in the ale.)

Me–I like all brands, but my favorite is Guinness Stout.

Marvin walked me into the noisy room and put me in crossties. A man called a blacksmith lifted my legs and pounded the bottom of my hooves. At first I jumped, for it felt strange.

Then he took my feet and cut away some of my hoof. It didn't hurt for a horse's hoof is comparable to a human's fingernail.

Next, the farrier took a piece of iron the shape of my foot, clapped it on, and drove nails through the shoe into my hoof. I can't say it was pleasant, but it didn't really hurt. Walking back to my stall my feet felt very heavy and stiff, but I got used to it.

The next morning Marvin introduced me to racehorse equipment. He slid a crupper under my tail and placed a heavy leather strap around my stomach called a harness. When he tightened it, I grimaced.

Then he put a bridle on my head with sidepieces called blinkers, and blinkers are indeed what they were for I couldn't see on either side--just in front. I wasn't fond of not seeing around me, but I did what he wanted. Eventually, Marvin changed my headgear improving my vision so I no longer bumped into the horse in front of me—a bad habit I had acquired.

After I was harnessed Marvin hooked me to a jog cart and off we went. I wasn't sure exactly what to do, but saw other horses that seemed to be enjoying it. Some were trotting, others paced, while a few galloped and played more than worked.

One colt bucked like a bronco, ejecting his driver and barreled until someone caught him. Thankfully, nobody got hurt!

Both Marvin and Cathy sat on the cart, but it didn't bother me for I was a big boy and could easily carry the weight.

As we passed horses one whinnied, *"What the heck are they doing to us?"* Another answered, *"We're jogging. It's what we're supposed to do."*

One yearling jumped sideways almost hitting me, but Marvin steered us out of harms way. We went around the track several times before going back to the barn.

"How was the big boy?" a groom asked.

"I'm pleasantly surprised. Gunner was a pro out there. Nothing seemed to bother him. I like him a lot," Marvin said.

After Cathy removed the equipment she gave me a warm sudsy bubble bath. Whatever she put in the water smelled good. She washed me different than Karen, for Cathy massaged me. She even washed the bottom of my feet, under my tail, and in between my legs–not missing one inch!

When I was dry we passed a mirror where I caught a glimpse of myself.

Damn! I shined like a new copper penny and my mane and tail were smooth as an Asian woman's hair.

As I strutted to my stall Pretty Woman nickered, *"My, my, my! You are a handsome thing. And you smell sooooooo good."*

Marvin passed by and heard us. *"What's all this commotion? If I didn't know better I'd say these two horses are talking to each other, Cathy."*

"Come on boss. I know horses are smart–but talking!" she laughed.

"Hey Cath, this horse is special! Remember–he dances–so perhaps he can talk?"

I heard them and told Molly, *"Why is it so hard for man to understand how smart horses are? I'm not the first horse that talked. Remember Mr. Ed, the talking horse? He even had his own television show!"*

"Maybe someday you can have your own show, Gunner. The Gunner Variety Show, and you can sing and dance," Molly laughed.

Each week a school bus came to the barn carrying small children. This was my favorite time and I counted the days until my little friends came, for I just adore kids!

Despite my massive size, I was the class favorite. The children brought carrots, peppermints, and apples; and one girl gave me a red Jolly Ball.

Marvin demonstrated the correct way to brush and groom a horse, and guess who he used as the model? Yep--It was Me!

The kids were in awe of how big I was, yet how gentle. They would take turns brushing my legs and tail–for they couldn't reach any higher.

"Gunner is such a ham when it comes to children. He will make such a wonderful riding horse someday," Marvin told Cathy.

I heard them and snorted, *"Listen here–I lovvvve kids and would love to go home with one, but riding–nope! Ain't gonna happen to this boy!"*

No horse is perfect. We all have quirks and idiosyncrasies. Mine was I didn't want anyone sitting on my back and have been that way since I was born!

When we were weanlings Bill got us accustomed to having something put on our backs, such as a saddle or harness. The others didn't seem to mind, but when he came to me, I bucked and squealed.

I don't know why I'm that way. Perhaps I'm ticklish, or it's a pet peeve, (no pun intended) but I don't want NO ONE or NO THING on my back! EVER! Thank God I wasn't born a thoroughbred or I would have been in serious trouble!

It freaked me out to see *anyone* on top of a horse. This caused a real problem—especially on the racetrack–for there's a person called an outrider whose job is to make sure all horses and drivers are safe on the track. If there's an accident or runaway, the outrider has to capture and return the horse safely to the barn. She does this while sitting on top of her horse. It's not an easy job for the safety of both the human and horse is in the outrider's hands.

I still remember the first time I saw an outrider–I galloped off the track and into the paddock. It took time to overcome, but eventually I did.

Marvin gave his horses Sundays off as most trainers do, for we all need at least one day a week to relax. During those days grooms would ride horses on trails behind the barn.

One day Marvin tried to get on my back. He pulled a chair alongside, climbed up and attempted to sit on me. I didn't know what he was doing, but I didn't like it.

I let him lay across my back, but when he tried to sit up, I threw him off. That was the last time anyone tried to ride me.

Chapter Six

THE LIFE OF A RACEHORSE

When You Are On A Great Horse, You Have The Best Seat You Will Ever Have

Horses need regular check-ups just like people. Once a year we visit the equine dentist, get a physical from the vet, and have our hooves trimmed by a blacksmith monthly. (Like a person trims his nails)

One day I had trouble eating my grain and was quite miserable. I love to eat and I'm not one to leave a morsel so when Marvin saw I was leaving feed he called the dentist.

Unlike humans, horses teeth grow for the rest of their life. In fact, the changes that take place to our teeth help determine our age.

Horses teeth are made of materials that vary in hardness. This causes portions of the teeth to wear.

A foal will have 24 teeth: 12 incisors and 12 premolars; and when we're 2 to 2½ years we get our second set of permanent molars. An adult horse has 36 teeth: 12 incisors, 12 premolars, and 12 molars.

(Adult horse teeth are 4-5 inches long, but the majority remains below the gum line.)

Now that's a lot of choppers!

At 4 our canine teeth come in, and by 5 our permanent teeth are in. When we're 6-years-old our incisors will start to show wear and by the time we're 7, 8, 9, and 10–cups of the middle and corner lower incisors disappear.

When we're 11 our upper incisors disappear and when we reach 30, if we live that long, we'll have short, small teeth or nubs.

Unlike humans we can't get our teeth cleaned, so you'll never see pearly whites when we smile. And our teeth don't sit flat on each other as yours do, for our upper teeth hang over on the cheek side of the lower teeth and the lower teeth aren't in contact with the tongue side of the upper teeth. (Get it?)

Some horses are born with 'a parrot mouth', which is a misalignment between the upper and lower jaws of a horse. This results in a faulty bite with the upper and lower teeth failing to meet correctly. (Similar to an overbite in humans)

But there are no braces for us!

Unfortunately, my wolf teeth didn't fall out when I was six-months-old like they were supposed to and this was the reason I had a hard time chewing my grain.

When the dentist discovered my wolf teeth were intact he pulled them. Although he gave me a sedative, it still hurt like hell!

Several yearlings had caps removed to make room for their permanent teeth. Dr. Mac also 'floated' all the horse's teeth in the barn.

(Floating means removing or repairing irregularities so we can chew our food.)

He was gentle, making my first time with a dentist as pleasant as possible, but I hated that thingamajig he put in my mouth.

So you see, good equine dentistry plays an important part in maintaining a horse's health throughout his life.

———

Every two months Marvin wormed his horses. I know that sounds gross, but sometimes horses get worms, just like dogs and cats. There are many types of worms that horses get, such as small strongyles, (the most common) large strongyles, roundworms, pinworms and tapeworms. In fact, horses can come in contact with over 150 different parasites.

How do we get them, you ask? Horses typically get these wiggly parasites from being in contact with fecal material. This is common in horses that graze in the field or are fed on the ground.

The eggs of the worms are ingested from infected pasture and develop inside the horses guts or lungs. If not treated, worms can damage a horse's intestines and other organs.

If a horse is infected with worms they will show signs, such as weight loss, scratching, poor coat or have a potbelly.

Marvin wormed his horses by putting a tube of paste in our mouth. Although it tasted really bad, it was totally painless.

———

Once a month every horse had an appointment with a blacksmith I called "Pedicure Day." After the first time getting my hooves done, it wasn't so bad–you just had to stand there awhile, but it goes pretty fast.

The blacksmith played country music, so of course I would start to dance—which really ticked him off.

When he was done, my feet were so clean. It's like when you get a manicure and they remove the dirt from under your nails and polish them. The blacksmith trims and cleans our hooves and polishes them with some shiny gooey stuff.

And of course the best were "spa days"–when we get special baths and rubbed downs. I felt like a million bucks when Cathy was done massaging me.

If a horse has a problem with his vision it can be hard to detect, for there is no equine optometrist, contacts, or glasses for equines.

And despite what you think—we are NOT colorblind. We can't see the color red, but we can see blues and greens; so the orange carrot you give us might appear green to us!

And horses see much better in the dark than humans because our eyeballs have more of the structures that pick up light.

Horses also have many of the same ailments as people, such as back problems.

I'm a big horse and large horses tend to throw their backs out more than small ones. One time when I was rolling, my back slipped out of place. Marvin called a chiropractor when he saw I wasn't standing properly, and believe me, it's damn agonizing when a horse hurts his back!

Back pain in horses can be notoriously difficult to isolate and treat.

Despite the popular myth—a horse's back is not actually designed to carry a load–and we weren't designed to carry humans on our backs. (See, I told you so!)

Therefore, a horse's spinal health is crucial to his function as a riding horse.

When our back is misaligned it is extremely painful and types of lameness can be attributed to spine and joint dysfunctions.

There are various symptoms a horse will show when this happens, such as: difficulty bending or flexing–back or neck pain—swishing their tail–head tossing–rooting–stiffness–and they won't stand on three legs when getting their hoofs trimmed.

A chiropractor can help us—just like they help you. The goal is to restore the spinal column's normal movement and function to promote healthy neurologic activity.

Marvin called Dr. Sue the equine chiropractor. She put me in crossties and used manual force on certain points of my back. When she hit 'the spot' I let out a squeal and dropped to my knees.

After an hour of applying pressure to various areas, I felt like a brand new horse and was pain free!

Bless that woman!

So you see, it's important horses get regular physicals, too.

Chapter Seven

MY FIRST RACE

When People Say 'It's Just A Horse', They Just Don't Understand

After training five months, the snow melted and temperatures rose so Cathy removed, washed, and packed away all the horse's blankets.

The hair on a horse has a different texture than humans and other animals. For the ones who had really thick hair, a man came and body clipped them. This helped reduce time to cool down and made grooming easier.

It didn't hurt, but it was a little scary. I think the noise was the worst part for it sounded like a nest of bees.

A lot happened that winter. Several horses left for they either got injured training or too immature to withstand the rigors of racing at the tender age of two.

Statistically, approximately 75% of horses make it to the races at two. So many things can and do happen while training, such as: injuries from pulling a suspensory, tendon, or hairline fracture. When this occurs, depending on the severity, the horse must be stopped and rested or perhaps undergo surgery.

Like people horses get colds, which can turn into pneumonia causing inflammation of the lungs. Any kind of upper respiratory infection can lead to pneumonia in horses.

This most commonly affects foals and young horses. When that happens it may require a trip to Ohio State University for medical care.

Treatment consists of antibiotics and fluid therapy and if not treated quickly it can be fatal. Sadly, this happened to my friend, Captain Jobe.

Thankfully, Pretty Woman and I survived the intense training, but a few walking wounded were sent to the farm for R&R. It was sad saying goodbye for we were family and looked out for one another.

One day, men called Amish came to the barn seeking expendable horses. They bought horses that were not racetrack sound or fast enough and made them buggy horses. I vaguely recalled hearing the word 'Amish' before, but couldn't remember when or where.

After talking to Marvin and looking at several horses, the men purchased Jolly Rodger and Susie Q.

When they walked on the trailer, Cathy cried.

"It's okay, Cath. You know Susie will be a mama, so she'll have a good life," Marvin said.

"But what about poor Rodger? They'll work him to death in the field, and he's still a baby! Why did his owner sell him to them? Couldn't he have been a riding horse or perhaps a jumper?" she cried.

"You know all horses can't have an easy life. I wish I had the money to keep them all, but it's just not economically possible. Hopefully, the family that bought Rodger treats their horses as prized possessions. They may use him only to drive to church on Sundays or the market."

"*Did you hear that Pretty Woman? I hope we don't get sold to those people. We better race well so they keep us here.*"

"*I know. I don't want to pull a buggy the rest of my life,*" she said.

June 19, 2004

<u>Springfield, Illinois</u>

It was June 19. I sensed something was about to happen for Marvin and Cathy paced the floor and stared at the clock on the wall.

It was an exceptionally muggy day, so fans were placed in front of the stalls to help cool the horses.

I heard Marvin say, "*It's a good thing Gunner drew a three hole in the race*"–whatever the heck that meant?

Several weeks before my first race Marvin took me behind a funny looking thing attached to the back of a pick-up truck.

He put my nose right on the gate and kept it there until the car sped away, then steered me to the hub rail behind the other horses.

Marvin said he wanted to teach me to "sit in a hole." I didn't understand what he was talking about because there were no holes on the track!

One day jogging a horse beside me tripped and fell. Since I wore blinders I couldn't see, but heard him. I over reacted, veered off the track and dumped

Marvin into a ditch. I returned to the barn without Marvin and waited by my stall for his return.

Thank God he had a sense of humor, for when he walked in the barn he was covered with mud from head to toe.

It was fun racing other horses but I was less than thrilled with the whip Marvin used when asking for speed. He didn't beat me, but when he wanted to go faster he'd flick the whip over my rump.

Afterwards he would apologize, *"Sorry Gunner, but I had to get your attention for you have a short attention span. When you're in a race you can't get lazy or the driver will have to wake you up and believe me they will be a lot harder on you than I am, buddy."*

The morning of the race Cathy didn't feed me breakfast, which ticked me off. She gave me a little hay, but passed me when dumping feed.

After loading the race bike and equipment on the trailer Marvin pulled the truck alongside the barn and walked me in the trailer with Molly.

"You know Molly can't go to the paddock," Cathy reminded him.

"I know, but at least she can ride with Gunner, for she keeps him calm," Marvin replied.

We drove several hours before stopping at a gated entrance. A man directed Marvin where to go. I heard a lot of noise and saw funny looking objects going around and around–which I later discovered were amusement rides and this was a county fair.

After I unloaded, Marvin walked me to an area where horses stood in open stalls and put me in slot #3.

I don't know why, but I started getting butterflies in my stomach. At first I thought they were hunger pains, but Pretty Woman told me she got them too before she raced. They weren't real butterflies of course; it was just the apprehension of what might happen next.

My driver, Richard, checked my equipment and consulted with Marvin a few minutes.

All those months of waiting and wondering what it would be like were over. It was now time for my first race!

This was totally different than the day I qualified, for today a lot of screaming people were in the grandstands.

Damn–those butterflies were there again!

After Marvin warmed me up I broke out in a lathered sweat. My adrenaline was pumped and I was psyched to finally become a racehorse.

My groom sponged me and covered me with a blanket to keep me warm until it was race time.

The paddock judge informed the horsemen:

Four minutes until post…. Marvin checked my equipment again.

I stood there like an old pro, while other horses acted up.

The horse next to me was pawing and got on my nerves, while another reared in crossties, almost breaking loose.

Although I was a bit unnerved I kept my composure.

Three minutes until post*.*... Marvin tied something around my tongue called a tongue-tie to keep me from biting or swallowing it during the race. It was wet and my tongue felt funny, but I knew it was for my own good.

Two minutes until post*...* Now I was really psyched.

I thought, *"Come on...let's get this party started!"*

The paddock judge called the horses to the track. The time had come!

Marvin and I had practiced what to do in 'post parade,' so I knew the routine. It's like dancing with a partner. He leads and you follow.

And it was true, for my driver told me what to do through my bit and lines, and I followed!

It was Post Time!

A man in a truck with a gate attached said, *"Drivers, turn your horses."*

Seven horses were guided to their designated positions behind the starting gate. When the gate opened, a few horses galloped–which is known as breaking stride.

I got away 6th and then moved to 5th on the outside. Down the stretch Richard showed me the whip and I knew what to do–it was time to accelerate.

My mother's words rang in my head, *"When you race, give it all you have."*

I wanted to make her proud, so I dropped my head down and dug in.

The announcer yelled, *"It's Mandala Quest in front by four. They reached the ¾'s in 1:32.1. And Gun-It is moving on the outside–now fourth, now third, as they reach the finish line in a time of 2:00 2/5."*

I passed several horses in the stretch and finished in third place–a neck and nose behind the winner. When I got back to the barn, Marvin was there with a big grin on his face.

"You did great, big boy! You finished third with a last quarter in 27.3. The gentle giant is a racehorse!"

After my bath Marvin walked me on the trailer and fed me hay. Molly was lying on the floor looking exhausted as if she too had just raced.

"I was scared, Gunner, but I'm so proud of you," she said before falling asleep. *"Boy, you were flying in the stretch!"*

When we returned to Sportsman Park, Marvin unloaded the equipment, put Molly and me in my stall and Cathy brought us dinner. Boy, I was ravenous for I hadn't eaten in almost 24 hours.

Cathy had mixed a special blend of warm bran mash, diced with carrots, apples, and a touch of honey. It was the best meal I ever had and thought, *"Racing ain't bad after all."*

I was pretty laid back, both in the barn and on the track. I always did what was asked and never gave anyone a problem. They said I was a "model" racehorse.

Cathy was right for if I had one mean bone I could be dangerous, but it just wasn't in me. The funny thing is, as mellow as I was, when I got behind the gate I turned into someone else.

Maybe it was my alter ego, but in a race I was anything *but* calm--I was competitive, ambitious, and racy!

Like a good athlete, I didn't want to just race better than the other horses—I wanted to do it *different*, and the lessons Marvin helped me overcome the challenges of racing.

1) To play the best of my ability.

2) To follow the KISS principle: "Keep It Simple Stupid." In other words: not to overthink during the race.

3) Expect it to be hard.

4) Win the mental game.

He said if I followed these steps–win or lose–I would feel great satisfaction, for in the end, that's all you can do!

As a two-year-old I raced 7 more times and ended the year a maiden—meaning I never won a race.

Many perks came with racing, such as the day after I got to spend in the paddock with Molly. We would lie in the grass soaking up the sun.

When Cathy brought me in I was bathed in warm sudsy bubbles that smelled like lavender and stood in a spa to cool my hot, tired legs. Next, she'd massage hot oil into my muscles that felt really good for it eased the tightness from racing.

After I was dry I'd strut back to my stall, head held high as I passed the mares. They'd curl their lips and take a big sniff before letting out a whinny.

"What a hunk," Voluminous said. *"You're my type of man."*

Pretty Woman got jealous and sulked, ignoring me, but eventually got over it.

"You really are a handsome horse. Tall, dark and handsome–that's you, Gunner," she said.

Now get this straight–horse racing is not all fun and games for us four-legged athletes. Racing is about gambling and that's what racehorses are bred to do–entertain patrons, because they like gambling on us.

But people have no clue what we go through and what goes on 'behind the scenes.'

The majority of trainers take good care of their horses and we show our gratitude by racing our best. But there are exceptions for some trainer's only care about themselves and saving a dollar by feeding cheap grain, poor quality hay, and bedding.

Horses prefer a clean bed of straw, but some trainers use insufficient bedding, thus we have to sleep on a hard, cold dirt floor.

I don't want to seem like a crybaby, but how would you like to sleep in a dirty bed with no covers and have bugs or an occasional rodent run over you?

And can you believe some trainers don't bathe their horse after exercising or racing? I observed this when horses down the shed row were put away dirty after they raced! Not a bath or even brushed! The equipment was removed and the horses were thrown in their stall sweaty and soiled!

I heard a groom call this "cold pack." I felt sorry for those horses, but there wasn't a damn thing I could do. Luckily Marvin is good to his horses as are the majority of trainers.

Just like in any type of business there are good and bad apples and horseracing is no different. I just wish owners, trainers, and fans would appreciate us for what we go through to become a racehorse.

Chapter Eight

UNDERSTANDING A HORSE

The History of Mankind Is Carried on the Back of a Horse

Horses aren't hard to understand and are more like humans than they are different. Despite our stoic nature we are soulful animals and there is something spiritually soothing about being close to us.

Health professionals say horses can reflect a person's emotions to bring relief from addiction and stress. This is one reason horse therapy has gotten rather big.

Bringing horses together with children who have emotional disorders has had startling results. Children with autism and ADD often struggle to communicate—but when they are with a horse they can achieve so much!

You ask how? Well I'll tell you. Horses react as a mirror to the person who is with him. We are prey animals, so we want to feel safe. We become fearful if we're with someone who's aggressive, noisy, disrespectful, or too controlling. On the other hand, if the person makes requests rather than demands, the horse will begin to cooperate for we are always looking for a leader.

The horse is an emotional animal. Our eyes reveal a great and powerful soul, so the expression, "The eye is the window of the soul" is true for both humans and animals.

Bet you didn't know the eye of the horse is one of the largest of any land mammal and both the strengths and weaknesses of the equine's visual abilities should be taken into consideration when training us?

As far as racehorses–you'll hear a trainer who is looking for a horse with 'a special eye'. Some seek large wide-apart eyes, while others a calm and peaceful eye, and most will stay away from a horse with 'a white eye' believing they will be harder to break and train.

———

Horses are nothing new. In fact, they have been around for a mighty long time! We evolved over 50 million years ago from small-toed animals to the big, beautiful single-toed horse we are today.

Humans began domesticating horses sometime between 4,000 and 3,000 BC. It could be both the domestication process, as well as the personal experiences of individual horses, that have influenced the way horses recognize and respond to human signals.

Communication is the key and primary way humans connect with horses; whether by pulling the reins of a bridle, squeezing your legs against a horse's side, or just talking to us–it's not rocket science.

Like most animals, horses communicate more through gestures and expressions than vocal cords. The ability to read and understand what a horse is telling you is what sets great trainers apart from others. These so called "horse whisperers" get so much more out of us than those who treat us cruel.

Chances are you'll understand what we're saying by our gestures and posture. We nicker when you bring us things we like—especially something good to eat.

Because people rely so much on verbal communication it's only natural to focus on horse's vocalizations when trying to figure out what he's saying.

Watch us closely. When a horse's ears are forward, he's alert. When his ears are pinned back close to the neck, he's angry and most likely will kick or bite.

A cocked hind hoof means we either don't want to be bothered, or perhaps we're not feeling well.

The position and movement of a horse's head are easy to see and you can tell a lot about his mood and what he's thinking.

When our head drops it's a sign we're relaxed and feeling good, and if we see or hear something our head will elevate.

When we're scared we'll spread our front legs out to the sides and lean back a little. And when we paw—something a lot of us do, it can mean several things.

Pawing is a natural behavior, but when a horse paws continuously he is trying to tell you something. If we're bored or impatient we'll paw letting you know we're tired of standing or perhaps we're in pain.

But when we strike–Watch out! This is very dangerous and if you're lucky you'll walk away with only a bruise for a strike can shatter a human's bone.

By observing our expressions and gestures you'll better understand what we're trying to tell you.

Horses have always been instrumental to man as it was the first thing that allowed man to travel faster than his two legs could carry him on land.

So you see, the horse has had a huge impact on the world since the beginning of time–everywhere– and on every aspect of life.

Yep, we are the unsung heroes of the world. All my equine relatives and me!

Chapter Nine

MY RACING CAREER

Horses Are Proof God Loves Us

During my racing career I started 104 starts; accumulating 6 wins, 9 seconds, 15 thirds, and amassed a total of $25,984.

I raced primarily at Illinois tracks such as Maywood, Sportsmans Park, and Balmoral. I also raced at several fairs.

Over the years I had many different drivers–some more aggressive than others. Like many of my fellow racehorses there were times I was forced to race tired or sore. My legs were weary from injuries, but I gave it my best every time.

And we get upset stomachs, too, but can't regurgitate (vomit) like humans. It's physically impossible for horses to throw up.

The reason is our esophageal sphincter is stronger than other animals and we're unable to open that valve from the stomach. This can cause us to colic—but it's a different colic than colic in human babies.

I saw a lot that winter I wish I hadn't.

My girlfriend Pretty Woman was involved in a bad wreck and euthanized. I thought I would never get over it, and in many ways I haven't.

Thankfully, the track was far from my stall so I didn't see the accident. I heard the sound of an ambulance and a lot of people crying. Our groom, Gary, brought the mangled race bike back to the barn with Marvin following.

Cathy and Marvin embraced as they cried and wouldn't look at me, avoiding eye contact the entire day. When Pretty Woman didn't return to her stall I knew something terrible happened, but it wasn't until the next day when I heard people talking that I understood.

Then my best friend, Molly, a beautiful Shetland pony who had been my constant companion since losing my buddy Running Boy, died in her sleep one night.

I never realized how attached to a pony a horse could get. I thought I'd have wanted another horse as my buddy, but the minute I met Molly I loved her. How could you not? She was the sweetest little thing. Being that horses and ponies are both intelligent animals, bonding between the two is almost a done deal.

When I traveled anywhere in the trailer Molly would lie by my feet. We ate together, slept together, and played together. So when I woke that morning stretching my legs, making sure I didn't kick Molly and she didn't move, I snorted and whinnied trying to wake her, but she lay perfectly still.

Marvin knew she had crossed the Rainbow Bridge, (Animal Heaven) but I had no idea. I thought she was sleeping until they wrapped her in my horse blanket and carried her out of the stall.

I cried for days. Yes, horses mourn, too!

The loss was unbearable. I think I miss her more than I miss my mother for Molly and I went through everything together. She never complained, left my side, and could never be replaced for she was one-of-a-kind.

Several months after Molly passed away a mare named Cleopatra came into my life. She had me at the first whinny.

Cleo—as I called her—was jet black with a tiny white shaped heart on her forehead. She was a southern belle from Georgia with the cutest accent. The day I met her, Jason Aldeans song, 'She's Country' was playing on the radio.

I started singing:

"You boys ever met a real country girl?
I'm talkin true blue, out in the woods down home country.
She's a hot little number in her pick-up truck
Daddys sweet money done jacked it up.
She's a party all-nighter from South Carolina
A bad mamma-jamma from down in Alabama,
She's a ragin Cajun, lunatic from Brunswick
Juicy Georgia peach
With a thick southern drawl, sexy swingin' walk."

Cleo completely ignored me, but the other mares in the barn swooned.

When Marvin turned us out, Cleo played hard to get. You know the way females are–they really want you to chase them, but act like they're not interested.

When I got within two feet, Cleo let out a blood-curdling squeal that could wake up the dead. She pinned her ears, swished her tail, spun around and fired!

She never physically hurt me, but my feelings were crushed for I had never been treated that way before.

It took a month before Cleo finally caved in. One day when I was grazing, I felt a gentle nudge. She began nipping my shoulder and worked her way up my neck.

That was it!!! I was in love with my sweet Georgia peach!

From that day on we were inseparable–until she fractured her coffin bone and was sold to that group of bearded men with funny trousers.

Needless to say, I was devastated when they took her away.

I cried for days and wrote her a letter as tears rolled down my face.

"My southern Peach–'Meeting you was fate. Becoming your friend was a choice, but falling in love with you was beyond my control.

Until we meet again—It is better to have loved and lost, than never to have loved at all!"

During my career I wanted to please and be a good racehorse. Unfortunately, I was involved in several nasty accidents.

One time a horse in front fell causing me to throw my driver and take off running. The outrider was trying to do her job and catch me; but remember--I didn't like seeing anyone sitting on top of a horse.

When she got near me I turned and ran the opposite way, dragging my mangled sulky behind. I must have run three miles before she finally caught me. Luckily, no one was seriously hurt.

I raced until I was seven-years-old. Along the way I sustained many injuries, but somehow always came back to race. I dropped a suspensory, had excessive scar tissue on my tendons, and suffered a sacroiliac joint dysfunction.

Marvin commented, 'he couldn't believe what a big heart I had'–meaning no matter how badly I was hurting I tried my best.

When my performances began deteriorating I knew my racing days had come to an end.

Marvin told the vet, *"Doc, Gunner's legs are no longer holding up. He's doing his best, but just can't race like he used to. I hate to send him out on the track in pain, and there's nothing more I can do to help him."*

"I agree. I think it's time you pull his shoes, hang up his harness, and call his owners," Doc said.

I was now seven-years-old and although that's not old for a Standardbred racehorse, because of my injuries and afflictions, like any other athlete, I was done.

I prayed to God that somebody would want me as their riding horse or family pet and I could spend my golden years in a pasture full of green grass, but that was not meant to be.

When the trailer pulled up the next day and those men in suspenders walked in the barn I knew my life would not be easy from here on in.

Chapter Ten

AN UNWANTED HORSE

In The Quiet Light of the Stable You Hear A Muffled Snort, A Stamp of the Hoof, A Friendly Nicker. Gentle Eyes Inquire, "How are you my friend?" and Suddenly All Your Troubles Disappear

My first thought was that the men with bushy beards were there for another horse, but when Marvin took me out of my stall, I knew my fate.

I thought to myself, *"Didn't I race well enough?" "Is it something I did?"* or *"Am I just an old nag that nobody wants?"*

Cathy left the barn crying and even Gary the caretaker shed a tear. I discovered my owners no longer could afford me and as hard as Marvin tried to find a good home, it appeared no one wanted me.

I didn't blame them for I was nothing but a has been, who could no longer earn money, but I tried–I really did!

In my final races I was competitive until the ¾ pole and then the pain became unbearable. As I crossed the finish line last I heard "boos" coming from the fans. These were probably the same people I made money for at one time.

But racing fans are fickle and love only those they cash tickets on. You can win three races in a row and you're the king, but lose one and you're a "pig," "nag," and "has been."

Marvin tried his damnedest to keep me racing by rubbing my achy legs with liniments, but it was useless. My front legs were crooked and no surgery could repair them.

One day a woman came to the barn wanting a horse for her daughter to ride. When Marvin showed her me, she jumped back and said, "*Oh no. That horse is way too big for Alice.*"

He assured her I was a sweet, gentle horse, but the woman decided to buy Misty instead. I was happy for Misty, but what made her a better choice than me?

———

The day I left Marvin's barn was heartbreaking. It was painful saying goodbye to my barn family I lived with for 5 years. During that time I had seen many horses come and go.

Cathy and Marvin fell in love, got married, and had a son named Stan who I adored. He would come to the barn every day with bags of carrots. I'd gently take them from his tiny hands, knowing he was just a little tyke then thanked him by kissing his head. I was hoping to be Stan's horse, but I guess it wasn't meant to be.

Before the bearded men loaded me on the trailer, Marvin threw his arms around my neck and whispered, "*I love you buddy. Do what these people say and they will be good to you. I promise to come visit.*"

But of course he never did, just like I never saw mama again.

As I rode away in the rusty old trailer I prayed for God to watch over me.

PART TWO

Chapter Eleven

MY THIRD HOME

A Great Horse Will Change Your Life.
The Truly Special Ones Define It

My new home was located in the country. It was so different than the way my life had been before, for it was quiet and peaceful here. There were no automobiles or honking horns, no screaming obscenities in the barn, and no horses training on a racetrack--only buggy horses traveling on cobbled roads.

It was absolutely beautiful. The grass was emerald green and the trees and flowers were in full bloom.

The people that acquired me were called Amish. Amish are God-fearing people. Families and farms are their top priorities—second only to God.

Most didn't use tractors or other machines in their fields, instead they relied on a draft horse or team of horses to pull plows and other farm equipment.

In the past donkeys were bred to Belgians, resulting with the foal being a strong large mule. It was popular with some Amish, but other families didn't use the mules because they were forbidden by the Amish Ministers for being an inappropriate mix of donkey and horse blood–a creature not originally created by God.

Electricity and telephones were forbidden on the farm. The reason was because they interpreted linking with electrical wires as a connection with the world. (*The Bible tells them they are not to be conformed to the world. Romans 12:2*) Thus, they are less threatened by power shortages caused by storm, disaster, or war.

The Amish value simplicity and self-denial over comfort, convenience, and leisure. Having and raising children and socialization with neighbors are the greatest functions of the Amish family.

A person is more a member of the family than an individual and each family member has a job, a position, a responsibility, and a status.

The Amish population is rapidly growing and the numbers more than double every 20 years due to having large families.

Family is the foundation of the Amish way of life. The structure and traditions that seem to be taken from a page out of history have remained an integral part of the Amish culture.

The family that bought me was The Yoder's. The man of the house was Jacob and his wife, Hannah. They had three small children: Samuel age 5, Mary age 4, and Ruth the baby, 2-years-old. Although I loved them all, Ruth was my favorite.

She was the cutest darn thing I ever saw for she had just learned to walk. She would wobble as she plucked clover to feed me and would sometimes fall. When she did I'd trot over to make sure she was okay. I nudged her with my nose and nickered and she would get up and hug my leg.

It was real nice not having to jog every day—especially since my legs weren't what they were when I was a youngster. The wear and tear of years racing took its toll, leaving me with a bowed tendon, dropped suspensory, and excessive scar tissue.

Jacob felt sorry for me, thus my only job was driving the family to church on Sundays and Hannah to the market.

My legs were swollen so little Samuel would walk me to the creek to stand in the icy water. This cooled my legs and reduced the inflammation.

The other horses on the farm that worked the field by pulling heavy tractors were jealous of my easy life.

I overheard them talking, *"Why does that standardbred have it easy while we have to plow and pull the tractor?"* Billy the Percheron asked. *"I mean, he's almost as big as we are, so how come he has it easy?"*

"He's not a draft horse like us—maybe that's why," Greengo answered.

My new life wasn't so bad, for I was fed three meals a day, spent time grazing in the fields and worked only one day a week—if you call driving to church on Sundays to give thanks to the good Lord work.

The entire service lasted three hours. Although I wasn't allowed inside, I could hear the music and singing.

It wasn't country music, but nonetheless, heavenly.

Outside the church 20 horses were tied to a post, leaving enough slack to munch on grass or get a drink if needed. One Sunday as I waited for mass to end I heard a familiar voice call out, *"Gunner, is that you?"*

I'd know that sexy voice anywhere. It was my Cleo!

I turned my neck as far as the rope allowed and saw Cleo at the other end of the row. She looked the same as the last time I saw her, only a little thinner.

"Cleo! It's so good to see you. How are you?" I asked.

"I'm okay. Just tired. My family works me so hard. I plow twice a week and it's rather laborious. What about you?" she asked.

"I'm so sorry, Cleo. I only work on Sundays driving my family to church and once in a while I take the missus to market. I'm very lucky, I guess."

When service ended Cleo bellowed as she trotted away, *"See you next week, Gunner."*

I nickered back. *"See you, Cleo. Try to get some rest."*

Little Ruth gazed at us in awe.

"Look daddy, Gunner is talking to his friend," Ruth said.

"No honey, horses can't talk," Jacob laughed.

Chapter Twelve

A NEW TYPE OF LIFE

Horses—If God Made Anything More Beautiful, He Kept It For Himself

It took some time getting used to certain things. Little things like Marvin wore jeans to the barn while Jacob sported suspenders and a broad-brimmed straw hat. Cathy came to the barn in a t-shirt and shorts, while Hannah wore a long dress and bonnet.

Even the Yoder children dressed different than little Stan.

Stan wore shorts, tennis shoes and a t-shirt, while Samuel (a clone of his father) dressed in trousers with suspenders.

Mary and Ruth wore long dresses and a white bonnet like their mother. They looked like real-life porcelain dolls, but I thought how hot they must be–especially in the summer.

As far as recreation, at the training barn Stan buzzed around on a three-wheeler. Samuel and Mary were not allowed to have bicycles because they have pedals, so they'd ride around the farm on a wooden skateboard made by their dad.

Amish children don't attend regular school, but the ones of age go to a one-room house with a wood stove inside that keeps them warm in the winter.

When the children are young they spend the majority of the day studying and learning to speak Pennsylvania German, but at school they speak mostly English and German.

They are taught the basics of reading, writing, and arithmetic; however, the Amish also teach their children things they'll need to know to succeed in their Amish communities.

A typical day on the farm began at five o'clock in the morning.

There were no alarm clocks–they woke with the rooster's crow and began their duties for even the children had designated chores. The Yoder children were too young to attend school so they stayed at the farm and helped their parents.

Samuel fed the chickens and goats, Mary swept the floors and made the beds, and Ruth helped her mother collect hen eggs. After their chores were finished they played with toys that were simple and non-electrical.

The Amish have what's called The Ordnung–an unwritten code of conduct that stresses values of humility, obedience, and simplicity, and oppose any form of violence. I personally never witnessed abuse of any kind on their wives or children, but unfortunately, this did not hold up when it came to their animals.

Some Amish overworked their horses in the scorching sun, causing dehydration and colic. One time I saw a horse stumble and fall while pulling a family. The driver got off and beat the horse until he got up.

Others left their horses at a roadside farm or stores where they sell their products without water to drink for hours as temperatures climbed to the 90's.

Of course this didn't happen to all of us—just the unfortunate ones.

Horses are an important part of Amish life, so treating them unkind is stupid, but unfortunately, there still are some that have a "use-them-up-and-dump-them" attitude that is senseless and cruel.

Can you imagine life without sunlight, or eyes so thick with pus from an untreated infection you have to strain to see out of them? Maybe your teeth are rotted and fur has thinned from self-injury and starvation?

Your compatriots are infested with parasitic insects and the unquenchable itching says maybe you are, too. Again, I never experienced this type of cruelty, but many of my friends had.

One day taking Hannah to market a car containing several intoxicated young men flew by blowing the horn and screaming. Startled, I steered off the road, but managed to keep Hannah safe.

A mile ahead was another horse and buggy. A semi-truck was speeding the opposite direction so the car swerved and hit the horse and buggy. It was the worst thing I ever experienced and pray I'll never see that again.

The horse fell to the ground as the buggy overturned, ejecting a small child. The cart broke in half and a lot of blood was shed. I was in shock and couldn't move but somehow Hannah managed to turn me around and headed home.

I looked forward to Sundays for I got to see Cleo. We'd talk about how our week went and reminisced the good old days. She was my only friend since the other horses on the farm avoided me.

I noticed Cleo was losing more weight.

"I'm worried about you, Cleo. You're getting too thin," I said.

"Don't worry. I'm just tired, but I'll be alright," she whispered.

When she didn't come to church the next Sunday I asked one of the horses if he knew where she was.

"Didn't you hear? Cleo died. She had a heart attack while pulling a plow. What a shame! She was so pretty and sweet. I think she was only seven-years-old," he said.

"Dead! How she can be dead? I just saw her two weeks ago."

Depression set in and I refused to eat. I stood in the field by myself with my head down.

Another loss of a loved one! I don't think I could take much more.

Chapter Thirteen

HOME #4

A Dog May Be A Man's Best Friend, But The Horse Wrote History

I lived with the Yoder's for two wonderful years. I thought it would be my forever home, but unfortunately, it wasn't.

Jacob got pneumonia and was unable to work the farm. The bank foreclosed and he, Hannah, and their three children moved to Lancaster, Pennsylvania, to live with relatives.

Since he could no longer afford his horses, we were sold to different families. An Amish man from Chicago bought Billy the Percheron and me. We never did become what you would call buddies for Billy never got over his intense jealousy.

It was sad saying goodbye to the Yoder's–especially to Ruth, who was now four-years-old. She was a beautiful, sweet child and my best human friend. While the other horses buddied in the field, I stayed by myself waiting for Ruth to come.

Although Amish children are not allowed to play competitively with others, Ruth and I played ball. She would kick it to me and I would take it in my mouth and toss it back. Ruth thought this was the funniest thing and laughed and laughed.

Her favorite toy was a faceless doll she carried everywhere. I discovered a doll without a face is part of the Amish culture. The reason is in the Bible the Book of Deuteronomy forbids the creation of graven images, which means that people cannot create an idol with human characteristics, as only God can create humans. Another belief is that a doll with a pretty face will make the child vain.

When our new owner came for Billy and me, Ruth cried.

"Please father, can't Gunner come with us?"

"No honey, I'm sorry. Gunner has to go with the man."

Hannah was holding Ruth as she jumped from her mother's arms and ran into the house. When she came out she was holding her faceless doll, Mimi.

"Daddy, please let Gunner take Mimi. This way he will never forget me," she cried.

As I walked on the trailer, Jacob handed the driver the doll.

"Please make sure this stays with Gunner."

The man placed the doll alongside the hayrack and I smelled Ruth's scent all they way to my new home.

I never did forget Ruth and her doll went with me from home to home the next eight years.

Chapter Fourteen

BECOMING A PLOW HORSE

To Ride A Horse Is To Fly Without Wings

The livelihood of Amish depends strongly on a horse for they are very important to their way of life and vital tools to their lifestyle.

At my new home I immediately became friends with an 1800-pound Belgian named Buster who was pigeon-toed due to pulling heavy equipment before his bones were fully developed.

His spirit was broken and petrified of people.

But not all Amish are this way for there are good and bad people in every sector. Perhaps some horses don't get plush sawdust stalls and bubble baths, but are taken care of.

Most Amish horses are used to pull a "sulky" plow. The Standardbred horse, like myself, is popular among the Amish for we have the ability to canter, trot, or pace. We've already been broken to the cart, which makes us perfect candidates for hitching to an Amish family's buggy.

And most Standardbreds have an even disposition, which is important as Amish horses are often on roads with traffic. In addition, Standardbreds are purchased fairly cheap, for once we're no longer able to race some owners look to unload us.

The 'ideal' buggy horse is a 4-to-6 year old gelding with classic good looks. The Amish will pay anywhere from $800-$4,000 for horses. There have been times when they've paid tens of thousands of dollars for a foal with good pedigree; and as I mentioned earlier they love black trotting mares and will pay a hefty price for one.

They prefer dark horses because shedding hair won't show on their black clothes.

The American Saddlebred is another breed commonly used to pull a buggy. This is a fairly sturdy breed with a naturally flashy snapping gait.

Draft horses are also popular among the Amish. The most common breeds are the Percheron and the Belgian draft for both are powerful and hardworking.

While most Amish use a horse to work their farm, some buy horses to re-sell, breed, and break for racing clients. Some racehorses that are not fast enough are bought by the Amish for a second chance in life on the buggy scene.

I was shuffled back and forth to several Amish families the next eight years. By the time I no longer was worth anything to them, my legs were bowed and suspensories torn–but they never got my soul. No matter how hard they tried—they couldn't break my spirit!

I had faith in God that my time on earth wasn't quite over, and somewhere, someone would want me. Mama said I was born to do something great–but what?

Unfortunately, after life as a race and plow horse I ended up in a horses' worst nightmare: the kill pen!

Chapter Fifteen

THE KILLPEN

God Forbid That I Should Go To Any Heaven In Which There Are No Horses

As I stand in this rusty old pen crowded with several horses, my life flashes before me. I'm now 16-years-old and wonder what I did to end up in this horrific place?

I know I wasn't a stakes horse or earned hundreds of thousands of dollars—but I tried and gave it my all every time.

I'm not alone for other horses are here with me. There's another Standardbred and three thoroughbreds, all waiting for whatever it is they're planning to do with us, and for some reason I don't think it will be pleasant.

Although I don't look nearly as bad as the others, I look nothing like I did when I was racing. My ribs now show, my fur is thin and drab, and my legs look like they've been through a war—and lost!

My front legs bend and toe in, my sacroiliac is extremely sore, and my suspensory is thickened from scar tissue.

After living with the Yoder's, I was sold three times to different Amish families.

The first was when Billy and I became plow horses. He was bigger and stronger and could endure the work much easier.

I lived at that farm for two years before being sold to a family in Ohio where I became a buggy horse. It wasn't so bad, except I was on the road more than the barn or field.

They fed and took good care of me, but it was strictly business. No one took an interest in me since the Yoder's. They treated me like I was family–something I haven't experienced since.

I long for someone to love, but to my new owner I was a mere object they worked very hard.

Many days I was forced to wear uncomfortable equipment I can only describe as dreadful. The bit in my mouth hurt my tongue and jaw so badly it would bleed and ulcerate. I'd throw my head to let my owner know I was in pain, but he would either ignore or hit me with the whip.

When he died I was sold to a family in Pennsylvania who had six children. Unfortunately, I never got a chance to interact with them like I did Ruth.

Boy, did I miss her. The doll Mimi got lost somewhere in the mix while I was shuffled around. For the longest time I'd lay my head on that doll when I slept, for I could smell Ruth's scent on it.

Once again I became a Sunday horse riding the family to church. Although I'm a big boy, pulling eight people was a bit hard—even for me. Thus, my weary legs throbbed with pain. When I no longer could pull the buggy, the family purchased a Percheron and shipped me here.

I am now waiting the uncertain. As memories of mother, Cleo, Pretty Woman and Molly flash in my head, a tear runs from my eye for I miss them so and fear for my future.

PART THREE

Chapter Sixteen

SOLD!

The Love For A Horse Is Just As Complicated As The Love For Another Human Being ...If You Never Love A Horse, You Will Never Understand

During the next two weeks I was shipped to several kill pens where I witnessed many horrific and inhumane things.

Various breeds were crowded in one large pen. Standardbreds, Thoroughbreds, Ranch Geldings, Broodmares, Performance Prospects, and innocent young colts crammed together like sardines.

Several horses paced in lieu of not enough room to do anything else–bellowing to be heard–but nobody came. A Palomino tried to whinny but was unable to for her owner had her silenced by painful instruments in a surgical operation. My heart broke when she tried to call out for not a sound escaped. The horrendous inability of trying to do something we were bred to do was too much for me to take.

Broodmares were kept barefoot and pregnant year after year interspersed with painful pregnancies and babies for whom they could not nurse due to painful infections like mastitis of the breasts.

This was the life of many horses for what seemed like eons, only to end in a kill pen when no longer useful or wanted. No horse deserves to be here or suffer the horrific journey to slaughter.

I discovered there are well over 150,000 horses shipped across the border to Mexico and Canada every year. Unfortunately, for large horses like me I am worth more for they buy 'per pound.'

For those of you who don't know what a kill pen is, I will explain.

Kill pens are designed lots where horses traveling across the United States on their way to Mexico or Canada stop over to wait for their "delivery" date.

Can you imagine? Waiting for your hour of execution! It's similar to a human on death row!

Sorry to be so blunt, but that's exactly what it is! And you know something? You may think we don't know what's about to happen to us, but we do, and the waiting and anticipation is more than we can bear!

There are people known as 'kill buyers' who contract with 'meat buyers' and must fill a quota every month, like a car salesman has a quota of cars to sell.

Some kill buyers re-sell us in the auction parking lot for a quick profit of $200-$300! Again, we're not "objects," so PLEASE don't buy us for food!

Horses, as well as other animals, suffer from over breeding, over use, and over population. There are just too many horses out there, thus most live in unsavory conditions.

Many well meaning, and some not-so-well-meaning horse owners have no clue the fate that awaits us. "Out of sight, out of mind," I guess.

At the first auction I was sold for the price of meat. Luckily, the deal fell through and I was shipped here. Again, someone purchased me for meat price and I was left standing in the filthy pen, waiting to be shipped out with other horses.

I heard a woman named Mary Elena saw my photo and contacted a volunteer that rescues horses. She felt very strongly about buying me–not knowing if I was sound, lame, sick, or healthy. The woman told Mary Elena she was sorry, but I was already spoken for.

I stood in that filthy pen for weeks, but nobody came. The surroundings were beyond sanitary— even for an animal. It reeked of week-old manure and urine-drenched ground. Cobwebs covered the stalls and rats the size of large cats ran across our hooves.

The small amount of feed we were given was moldy, and our water buckets were often empty. One time I went to get a drink and saw a dead rat floating in the bucket, thus I went without water for an entire day.

I never saw horses in such poor condition, even those at the racetrack.

The mare's face was disfigured and her eye sockets fractured. The gelding had two broken fused knees. The thoroughbreds' reproductive organs had been ripped apart giving birth and were infected. All the injuries were caused by neglect and abuse by the hands of their owners or trainers.

Although I wasn't what you'd call 'a looker' at this time, I looked good compared to the others.

There was a pregnant thoroughbred that was unable to race due to a track injury. My heart broke for she was carrying a new life inside her.

If Mary Elena bought this mare she would get 2 for the price of 1. If I were looking to buy a horse, it would be this mare.

I would gladly take the mare's place so her unborn foal could live. Maybe it would have a better chance in life than I did. After all, I've seen and done it all in the sixteen-years I've lived on Planet Earth.

And there was a youngster standing in a corner who didn't look any older than two. He was a Palomino with a beautiful head who would have made a terrific show horse.

There were sorrels, bays, duns, blacks and greys. Thoroughbreds, Standardbreds, Quarter Horses, and Morgans; there was a horse for everyone.

A worker commented that 9 racehorses were meant to disappear but a Good Samaritan raised $10,000 and they were to be shipped to New Jersey that day.

Praise God!

He said people overlooked buying horses at an auction thinking they were dangerous, ill, lame, or old. Although this may be true in some cases, many are 'Diamonds in the Rough' who would make great pets, show, and riding horses for children.

Several weeks passed when a woman contacted Mary Elena saying there had been a clerical error and I wasn't spoken for after all and wondered if she still wanted me.

Mary Elena quickly said 'yes' and I was shipped to the New York Horse Sanctuary for quarantine with 3 other rescues: 2 standardbreds and 1 thoroughbred mare.

I had given up hope when the door opened and she walked in.

Chapter Seventeen

AN ANGEL IN BLUE JEANS

In Riding A Horse We Borrow Freedom

January 8 was a cold, wintry day. It was also the first day of the rest of my life. When the sanctuary door opened, an angel in blue jeans entered.

The brown-eyed girl walked up to my stall and gently touched me. I remember Cathy telling Marvin the first time he touched her she melted. Well, that's exactly how it felt when Mary Elena put her hand on my neck.

I can't explain it. It's an unbelievable feeling that starts from your head and travels to your feet. A tingly, indescribable sensation, and if you've never experienced it, I pray someday you do.

"Don't worry Gunner. I've waited a long time for this moment. I tried buying you before, but someone beat me to it. My heart was broken for the minute I saw you I knew you were meant to be mine.

But now you are, and despite all your physical ailments we're going to fix you up and make you the superstar you were born to be. We all have a purpose in life, honey, and God sent you to me to find out what that is," she smiled.

Can this be true? Am I dreaming? Am I really going to be free, or is this some kind of sick joke? What does this woman want with me? I'm a worthless, broken, sixteen-year-old gelding that can't race or work land.

I can't breed a mare to give her a colt. She can't ride me for I won't let ANYONE on my back. So why in the heck would she want ME–a washed out has been?

Just then she turned, walked away, and left the room. My heart sank for I thought she had come to her senses realizing I wasn't worth the cost.

All my hopes and dreams crumbled. I was sad, but I didn't blame her for she could surely purchase a horse to better suit her needs.

I looked at the other three horses. They were frightened and unsure of what would happen next. I tried to be brave and let them know we were all going to be okay.

The thoroughbred was especially scared for she had been at the kill pen the longest and uncared for. I walked up, looked her in the eyes and whinnied, letting her know we were no longer at an auction, but at the sanctuary. We were some of the lucky ones saved from a cruel and early death.

Chapter Eighteen

FREE AT LAST

God Once Said, "I Need Someone Strong Enough To Pull A Cart But Gentle Enough To Love A Child, Smart Enough To Protect His Master And Passionate Enough To Love His Family. Someone With So Much Love They Can Lift The Spirits Of A Broken Heart".... SO GOD CREATED THE HORSE

After Mary Elena paid my $860 asking price, I was shipped and quarantined for one month. Every single day the young woman with long brown hair came to see me. There wasn't a single day she missed and I found myself anxiously waiting for her.

Of course I couldn't read the clock hung on the wall, but right after breakfast she would arrive.

I was grateful, but thought, *"Is that all I'm worth? Seven years racing my heart out with aching joints and eight years pulling heavy equipment and plows and I'm not even worth a lousy grand?"*

But like mama taught me early in life to be thankful for everything, and I was beyond ecstatic that someone rescued me.

Mary Elena walked up and said, *"Hi buddy. I hope you don't get sick of me because you're stuck with me. Pretty soon you'll be getting out of here and coming home with me."*

Every day she brushed me, cleaned and polished my hooves, and rubbed my legs with something that smelled good. I don't know why she was so good to me, but I liked it.

After the quarantine time was up, I was released to my new owner. Since she didn't have a bushy beard and wear trousers with suspenders so I hoped maybe it would be different this time.

Mary Elena walked me on the trailer, along with 2 other rescues, and off we went. I thanked God that someone saw me worthy enough to save and not end up as someone's meal!

———

It was a snowy Saturday in February when I arrived at the place that would become my forever home. Despite the cold temperatures a lot of people were gathered there—all waiting to see me.

At first I was cautious for why would anybody want to see me, a crippled old nag? But *something* told me not to worry for it would be different this time.

Maybe it was *'A Whisper From God'* or a *'Horse Hunch'*–but I knew my life was going to be okay.

Mary Elena put me in an extra large stall filled with clean straw, a bucket of fresh water, and the best darn hay I ever tasted. A short while later she brought me dinner. It was my favorite–warm bran mash!

I wondered how she knew it was my favorite?

When I was done eating–and I didn't leave one morsel–my belly was full. Physically and mentally exhausted from everything I had been through the past few months, I decided to rest. It felt good to be lying in a clean stall and not a dirty, musty one.

As soon as my eyes shut I drifted into an uneasy sleep and dreamt of mama.

We were grazing in a field of clover, but I wasn't a small colt—I was grown up and much taller than mama. She was still the prettiest thing I ever saw and was wearing a pink ribbon in her hair.

It was so surreal I kept blinking to see if she would be gone, but she was still there.

"Mama, is that really you?" I asked.

"Yes, baby. You are so tall and handsome. I heard about your racing career and I'm proud of you."

"I didn't do that good, but I tried every time, just like you told me to."

"Why didn't you ever come back to see me?" I asked.

"I'm sorry, honey, but I've been busy having babies. You have sisters and brothers now, but you are still my favorite," she said resting her head on my shoulder.

"I know you've had a rough life, Gunner. It broke my heart to see how you were treated and overworked, but I knew God was protecting you. Remember—He will never leave you."

"And now we're together again and we'll never be apart!" I smiled.

"Yes, but I can't stay. I live in Heaven now and have to go back."

*"No, please don't leave me **again**, mother,"* I cried.

"I must, but you will be there with me someday. Until then, Pretty Woman, Molly, and Cleo, said hello."

"They're all there? I want to go, too!"

"It's not your time yet. There is something very important you have to do here on earth."

"What is it? Please tell me," I begged her.

"I cannot, but you will find out soon. I promise you'll never again be mistreated, for God told me the rest of your life on earth will be wonderful.

So until it's your time to cross the Rainbow Bridge, never forget how much I love you, son.

And when you feel scared or alone, look up at the sky. You may not see me, but I'll be there. I will send you a sign letting you know I'm watching."

And then I woke up! Just like that!

Mama was there one minute and gone the next! I was really confused. Was I dreaming, or had she really been there with me?

I stood up, shook the straw off my body, and looked around. At first I didn't know where I was, but then I saw the roan mare that was rescued with me and remembered. I was happy to be out of the kill pen, but sad that mama had just been a dream.

I looked out my window and saw Mary Elena walking towards the barn. As she opened my stall door, we locked eyes.

"Good morning Gunner. I hope you had a good nights sleep. Today you are going to go outside and just be a horse."

As she led me out she stopped and picked something off the ground. It was a pink ribbon! It was the ribbon mama had in her mane!

"Oh, one of the girls must have lost her hair ribbon," Mary Elena said putting it in her pocket.

My heart filled with joy knowing mama really had been with me during the night!

Chapter Nineteen

MY FOREVER HOME

When I bestride him, I soar, I am a hawk: he trots the air; the earth sings when he touches it; the basest horn of his hoof is more musical than the pipe of Hermes.

William Shakespeare

There was two times in my life I thought I was in love. Once was with Pretty Woman and the other was Cleo.

I didn't exactly know how 'being in love' was supposed to feel, but I heard Cathy tell Marvin the first time he touched her she had goose bumps all over her body.

I believe this woman who rescued and saved me was my first 'true human love' for when she touched my neck, I felt tingly all over; and when we locked eyes, I melted.

Could this be true love? I wasn't sure if she felt the same way, but I hoped the feeling was mutual.

The next morning Mary Elena turned me out in a huge field. There were no other horses and in a way I was glad. Although I longed for a companion, I didn't mind being alone for a while.

It took some time to realize what I was supposed to do, for it had been years since I had been turned out. I forgot how to run, jump, play and just be a horse. I didn't have a sulky, buggy, or plow attached to me. I was free as a bird that had been locked away in a cage and had just been let out.

At first I walked slowly, taking in my new surroundings. Smelling the clean, fresh, crisp air was something I hadn't experienced in years.

There were several horses in another field watching my every move.

After a few minutes, it all came back to me. I ran, bucked, and leapt for joy. I galloped from one end of the field to the other. I was so happy I cried with joy, *"I'm FREE! I'm FREE! Look at me–I'm FREEEEEEEEEEEE!"*

The other horses started running, too.

"He's free! Mary Elena saved another one! May God bless this woman!" cried a bay mare.

A chestnut gelding trotted to the fence and hung his head over.

"Welcome friend. My name is Kirby."

"Hi Kirby. My name is Gun It, but you can call me Gunner," I bellowed.

A group of people had gathered taking pictures. I thought 'why in the heck would they want a photo of me?'

Was this really happening, or just another one of my silly dreams? I knew one thing for sure: I wasn't on a racetrack with aching joints, I wasn't pulling heavy equipment on a farm, and I wasn't in a kill pen waiting to be slaughtered.

I looked up at the sky and gave thanks to God when a few drops of rain landed on my nose. Funny, for it wasn't raining anywhere, but directly over me.

How could that be possible?

Just then a double rainbow appeared in the sky.

"Do you see that, Mary? It's only raining over Gunner. And there's a rainbow? How strange! How can this be? Mary Elena's friend asked.

"That's a sign everything is going to be alright," Mary Elena said smiling. *"And it's a double rainbow which is considered a symbol of transformation and good fortune in eastern cultures. This is an affirmation from God that Gunner is where he's supposed to be and everything's going to be okay."*

I shook my head trying to get the raindrops off, looked up at the sky, and saw a beautiful arch of colors form.

"Is that where mama lives? Is that where the Rainbow Bridge is—where all the animals cross when they die?" I thought.

It was absolutely breathtaking. Colors of pink, blue, and yellow formed a perfect arch. I squinted against the sun looking for the bridge, but didn't see it. I remembered mama telling me she would give me a sign. Was this it?

I was hoping to get a glimpse of mama, Pretty Woman, Cleo, and Molly, but couldn't see them. I longed to cross the bridge and be with my loved ones but like mama said, *"It wasn't my time yet."*

The next several weeks Mary Elena let me just 'be me.' She didn't make me work or do anything I didn't want to–just graze on the new grass sprouting through the ground.

Spectators showed up the same time every day to watch me play.

I'd roll in the grass, get up, jump, and hold my tail in the air as I trotted, showing off for my new friends.

They would laugh and giggle as I entertained them. Funny, but I wasn't hurting anywhere. For the first time since I could remember, I was pain free.

Every day my new owner brushed me before turning me out, doctored any scars I had with ointment, and covered me with a blanket when it was cold out.

I was bathed weekly and my hooves trimmed once a month.

My new owner and I were developing a deep bond, but I was still a bit skeptical for I had lost faith in man and afraid to trust anyone again. But for some reason, I trusted this woman. She took care of me like I really mattered.

I loved it here and prayed it would be my last home.

Chapter Twenty

MY NEW FRIENDS

A Great Horse Will Change Your Life. The Truly Special Ones Define It

Like the Beatles song, *"With a Little Help From My Friends,"* friends are special, not only to people, but also to animals.

Shortly after moving to my new home I met two horses named Kirby and Xena, who became my BFF's and remained so for the rest of my life.

Friends have a strong positive effect on you and play a huge role in your life. They make you feel good, help define your priorities, and support you through thick and thin.

They help you celebrate good times, provide support during bad times, prevent loneliness, give you the chance to offer companionship, and increase your sense of belonging and purpose. Friends also boost your happiness and reduce stress–and Kirby and Xena did just that!

We were quite different, but similar in many ways.

Kirby was a chestnut saddlebred gelding and Xena a Fresian mare.

Usually horses pair in two, so if there are three one may end up alone. But not us! The three amigos—the three musketeers–the three stooges. We were a team!

At first Mary Elena turned me out alone for she wanted me to get used to my new environment but after a few days she put Kirby with me.

She said, *"I'm going to see how Kirby gets along with Gunner. The poor thing doesn't remember what it's like to just be a horse. I really want the two of them to re-discover life together."*

Kirby cautiously walked into the paddock with his head held high. We sniffed each other and whinnied. As our noses touched, I let out a blow— my way of greeting.

I think I must have snorted too loud and scared him for he ran away, but within minutes he returned and nuzzled my neck letting me know we were friends.

During the day we'd run, play, and lie in the sun eating grass; and at sundown Mary Elena put us in our own stall.

Kirby was also a rescue Mary Elena rescued from the kill pen. He told me war stories, for he had been severely abused.

Kirby never made it to the races so the Amish Purchased him as a two-year-old. His family was not one of the nicer ones, for they worked the poor thing to the limit. Not in the best health because of severe arthritis and a broken pelvis he sustained while pulling a buggy, they shipped him to the auction for the price of meat.

After Kirby and I were together several weeks Mary Elena introduced Xena, a Fresian mare.

Bringing another horse to an established herd can really up anxiety.

When two horses are established and a third is introduced the newbie may or may not be accepted. A pair of horses will establish some kind of subtle or overt hierarchical arrangement, but Mary Elena wasn't concerned for Xena and Kirby already knew one another.

"Hi Xena. It's a peachy day out. Meet my new friend, Gunner," said Kirby.

Xena and I put our noses together and released a soft snort. At first she swished her tail disapproving, but after seeing I was no threat the three of us galloped off to find shade from the hot sun.

Mary Elena had adopted Xena to be a police horse after her owner became ill and was unable to care for her.

"A police horse? What is that?" I asked.

"That's a very important job," Kirby said.

"I patrol areas of the city, meet school children and help with crowd control at big city events," bellowed Xena.

"That sounds exciting, but dangerous. I could never do that! NO way!

"Where did you get the name Xena and what does it mean?" I asked.

"My mother named me that. It means 'a warrior.' In Greek mythology, Xena was an immortal horse, belonging to Achilles. In popular culture, Xena is the Warrior Princess."

"Wow! I never met a Princess before," I said in awe.

Every night before going to sleep we said our prayers and thanked God for protecting us and giving us a wonderful home. After praying, Xena would tell us a story. They were always about being brave and thankful for what she had.

She was a sweet mare and gentle soul who suffered from laminitis. Although I didn't have it, I heard Marvin explain to Cathy what it was.

"Laminitis is a painful disease that affects the horse's feet. Sometimes it comes from overfeeding the horse. In severe cases, the bone and the hoof wall can separate," he told her.

Elocutionist, a horse in Marvin's barn had a severe case and had to be euthanized.

"Ouch! I sure hope I never get that."

Living on Mary Elena's farm was pure heaven. My friends and I would run and play. Although I limped for my knees were bothering me, when I was with my friends I forgot the pain. We would jump like spry youngsters.

Mary Elena commented on how high I leaped and said she wasn't sure if she would be able to ride me because of my size.

"Ride me! No way. I mean I am really grateful for everything you have done for me, but there is no way in the world I will ever let you, or anybody else on my back!"

And my new owner discovered I didn't like walking through doorways, and–oh yea–I wasn't fond of men! But regardless of these little quirks, she accepted and loved me for who I was.

It was as if I had never had a previous life. The one filled with pain and heartache was now only a dream–a very bad one. Mary Elena and my new friends had given me a new outlook on life. I wasn't sure exactly what I was supposed to be doing, but it wouldn't be long before I'd find out.

Chapter Twenty-One

TLC—THE BEST MEDICINE

All I Pay My Psychiatrist Is The Cost Of Feed And Hay, And He'll Listen To Me All Day

I thought I'd seen it all at the racetrack, but at my new home I was introduced to things I hadn't dreamed existed.

One day Mary Elena brought a chiropractor to the farm. I remember seeing one at Marvin's, but forgot how good they can make you feel.

Mary Elena noticed I was stumbling and having trouble getting up and down for my back injury had flared. When Dr. Bob arrived I was put in crossties. He was holding some kind of strange looking tool. The chiropractor at Marvin's only used her hands, so I wondered how bad this was going to hurt.

Mary Elena sensed my fear and rubbed my neck.

"It's okay, Gunner. I promise this won't hurt. It will make you feel better. I will never have anyone do anything to you if it's painful. You've suffered enough for three lifetimes," she said in a soothing voice.

Dr. Bob performed a technique called a "high velocity thrust," which adjusted and realigned my spine. The whole procedure took about one hour and when he was done, Mary Elena walked me back to the field to be with my friends.

Dang–she was right–again! I felt so much better and was pain free.

I was surprised to see Dr. Bob make weekly visits. Mary Elena said they were follow-ups to help keep me in good shape. It appeared the times I was involved in race accidents, I injured my neck and back.

And like people, horses can develop arthritis from an injury or aging. In my case, it was both.

Not only did I have regular sessions with Dr. Bob, but Mary Elena also got me a masseuse. Can you believe that? I had my own personal masseuse!

I was introduced to Kevin one day after a chiropractic session. He was a blond man who talked with a funny accent for he came from a country called Sweden.

Kevin was a soft-spoken, gentle man. He was a horse masseuse (also known as equine massage therapist) who used different techniques to relieve stress and improve performances.

The arthritis had settled in my joints; thus, every morning I had trouble moving and my range of motion was restricted.

After examining me Kevin said, *"Gunner's longissimus dorsi's are extremely tight."*

"My what! What's he talking about?" I snorted.

He must have read my mind for he explained, *"When muscles become chronically tight, the fibers lie closer together. This constricts the flow of blood through the muscle belly. It's like stepping on a garden hose–it reduces the flow of water."*

"It's obvious this horse's body has been through many battles, and unfortunately, he was on the losing end.

He's also very big and now that he's older the arthritis is setting in."

"Do whatever you can to help him," Mary Elena said. *"I don't want him in any pain."*

For the next hour Kevin placed the palm of his hand on my funny sounding thing–(Longissimus dorsi) and pushed in gently, working his way down the muscle.

I jerked for at first it hurt. My back hollowed and I moaned.

Once again Florence Nightingale came to my rescue.

"Hang in there, Gunner. It won't be long now. You will feel soooooo much better when Kevin's finished," Mary Elena said. *"I promise!"*

And again, she was right! Was this woman ever wrong?

When Kevin was finished he said, *"I'm done, Mary Elena. This should do it, but it would be better if you would ride him a bit, cantering in both directions."*

"Unfortunately, Gunner has a phobia of being ridden. He has never had anyone on his back and most likely never will," Mary Elena replied.

RIDE ME! NO WAY! Don't forget I have humanophobia!

I just made that word up because a fear of horses is called equinophobia, so I have humanophobia–a fear of humans riding me.

The expression on Kevin's face was priceless and I knew what he was thinking.

"Can't ride him? Then exactly what is this horse good for? Why are you putting so much money into him if he can't be ridden?"

Funny, Kevin, I was wondering the same thing.

Chapter Twenty-Two

A NEW ME

Horses Lend Us The Wings We Lack

I was so happy with my new life. Mary Elena was an angel who truly loved me; and my horse friends, Kirby and Xena, were the best any horse could hope for.

We looked out for one another and were inseparable. The only time we were apart was when Mary Elena brought us in the barn at night.

Our stalls were next to each other so we would talk most of the night, until we fell asleep. We'd discuss our past life and situations we endured: the good times and the bad times. Unfortunately, the bad outweighed the good!

It was Kirby who usually fell asleep first. Boy, was he a snorer! He would moan, groan, and snuffle while he slept. Although he kept me up, I didn't have the heart to wake him.

He had lived a horrible life and was brutally abused by his owner. His family overworked him causing the road accident. One day while taking his owner to market, his weary legs buckled from under him, unable to go any further. He stumbled to the ground and couldn't get up.

His owner jumped off the buggy and whipped him mercilessly, drawing blood from his stifles. Broken and in pain, he was made to continue the trip to the market and back.

When they arrived home he was put away without a bath, his injury tended to, or the newly broken pelvis addressed. Unable to work or pull the buggy anymore, Kirby was shipped to an auction for meat price.

Mary Elena saw him standing by himself, a disheveled looking thing and her heart ached. Despite his swollen knees and fractured pelvis she purchased him and took him to the farm.

———

Several weeks went by before Mary Elena introduced a fourth horse into the field. She was a striking Clydesdale. The minute I saw her I knew I was in trouble! It just so happens that Travis Tritt was singing one of my favorite songs on the radio: "T-R-O-U-B-L-E."

My heart beat fast and I broke into a sweat. I must have looked like a big dummy for I stood there gawking with my mouth open. After a few minutes, I gathered myself and started singing, hoping to get her attention.

"Well I play an old guitar from nine till half past one,
I'm just tryin' to make a livin' watching everybody else havin' fun.

Well I don't miss much if it happens on a dancehall floor–
Mercy–look what just walked through that door.
Well hello T-R-O-U-B-L-E,
Tell me what in the world you doin' A-L-O-N-E.
Yeah, say hey good L double O-K-I-N-G
Well I smell T-R-O-U-B-L-E!"

Xena and Kirby started whinnying, which was their way of laughing–but the new horse ignored me.

I never saw a mare that size before. She looked different than the others, for long hair covered her hooves. I wasn't sure if they forgot to trim it, but it sure looked funny. Regardless–even with the untidy hoof hair, she was stunning!

Her name was Madison. She was a 6-year-old bay with a white stripe down her face. I'm a big boy–17 hands–so she had to be at least 18 for I had to look up to see her blue eyes and long eyelashes.

It was so refreshing meeting someone taller than I was—especially a female. Although she was big, she was quite timid and for the first few days Madison stayed off by herself in the field.

Mary Elena said Madison had been kicked in training school and was scared to be next to another horse. She was a PMU rescue who came with baggage, for she also had encountered troubles and poor past experiences.

It took several weeks, but eventually I won her trust. After she let me know it was okay to approach her, I walked up slowly and said, "Hi Madison. What a pretty name for a pretty mare."

She batted her big blue eyes and said, "You can call me Maddy."

We locked eyes and you could've stuck a knife in me for I was done!

I was in love AGAIN!

Just then I remembered something Dr. Seuss said, "You know you're in love when you can't fall asleep because reality is finally better than your dreams."

Yep, that is exactly how I felt about Maddy.

Chapter Twenty-Three

TIME FOR WORK

You Can See Beautiful Things That Make You Cry, However, None Of Them Can Match The Grace And Beauty Of A Horse In Freedom

I had been living at a place I called "Heaven On Earth" for two months. The weather was quite warm, so the horses stayed outside at night. The four of us sprawled on the grass--close enough we could watch one another--but far away enough to roll and stretch our legs.

We loved watching the stars light up the sky. That's when I would think of mama.

One morning Mary Elena took me out of the field and into the barn. She put me in crossties and removed several things from a wooden trunk. It was horse equipment, but nothing I wore as a racehorse.

Sensing my fear, she let me smell each piece and explained what they were. There was a saddle pad, a girth, and something called a saddle. She put them on me and walked around wearing the equipment. We repeated this every day for a week so I could get used to them.

On the second day Mary Elena hooked me to a long lunge line. We started out walking then advanced to a slow jog. She was surprised I was sound, despite my bent legs.

I went around and around in circles, pacing then trotting, while playfully bucking and kicking. Mary Elena laughed for it must have been some sight seeing a horse my size going in circles. I really enjoyed it, but have to admit I was getting a little dizzy.

The next few days she walked me over funny looking obstacles, tarps, and bridges. One day her girlfriend Eva came to help, for at this point Mary Elena needed a helping hand. I instantly liked the soft-spoken blond with a pretty smile.

When Mary Elena saw I was okay wearing the equipment she did something I thought I'd never see again–she attempted to get on my back!

She whispered, *"Hey buddy. Xena isn't feeling well and I'm hoping you can help us out. You see, I have to get my certification renewed at the police school and need you to step up to the plate."*

"It would mean the world to both of us, so if you can try, I promise to take it slow and be gentle."

Chapter Twenty-Four

BECOMING A
RIDING HORSE

A Horse Gallops With His Lungs, Preserves With His Heart, And Wins With His Character

Well, it was now or never! Although I swore I would NEVER let ANYONE on my back again, here I was letting Mary Elena. After all—I literally owed this woman my life, so this was the least I could do to repay her, no matter how scared I was.

She slowly climbed up on my back. At first I panicked and wanted to run as fast as I could! She sensed my anxiety and rubbed my neck until I relaxed and stopped flinching.

"Try to relax, Gunner. I won't hurt you," she said.

After several minutes, I collected myself. She didn't keep me out too long and I was thankful. When we were done Mary Elena took me back to the barn and removed the equipment. Kirby, Madison, and Xena were waiting in their stalls.

"How was it, Gunner?" asked Kirby.

"It wasn't that bad, was it?" said Xena. *"I really enjoy riding and hope you will learn to, too. Thanks a lot for stepping up to the plate to help me. I'm really in a lot of pain and I know how important it is for Mary Elena to get her re-certification. I know you will do just fine."*

The second ride was easier than the first, and by the third time I was riding in the field!

"I'm so proud of you, Gunner. I knew you could do it--we just had to convince you!" Mary Elena laughed.

At the end of the week she told her friend I was ready for the test.

TEST! I don't like the sound of that!

Mary Elena clipped, washed, wrapped my legs, and loaded the trailer with enough supplies for two weeks.

This was the first time I would be leaving my new home since moving here. I didn't want to leave my friends and was a little worried.

My mind started playing tricks on me.

Where was she taking me? She's not sick of me, and taking me back to the kill pen, is she? Would she bring me back here? Would my friends be here when I returned? What if she isn't pleased with my work--will she find another horse to replace me?

All these crazy thoughts played in my head as the truck pulled up to a sign that read, "Remount School."

Chapter Twenty-Five

REMOUNT SCHOOL

A Horse Is More Than All The Riches In The World

I was amazed at the number of horses enrolled at the school.

A total of 25 four-legged students had shipped in from the east coast.

Before unloading, Mary Elena prepared what would be my temporary home for the next two weeks, filling my stall with clean straw and a bucket filled with fresh water.

She was very protective and disinfected the stall with bleach before putting me in for she didn't know who had been there before.

Isn't she a doll?

When she took me off the trailer Mary Elena walked me to a grassy area to graze which helped me relax and get acclimated to my new surroundings.

It was now lunchtime, and boy was I hungry! She prepared bran mash and my favorite drink: apple juice water! I slurped that sweet liquid down and then relaxed in my stall.

An hour later she tied me to a hitching post, alongside other horses. This was nothing new to me for I had been tied to posts many times while living with the Amish.

I didn't understand why people kept walking up to look at me. I thought perhaps something was stuck in my mane, or on my face. Maybe I had a piece of straw in my nose, or bird droppings in my mane?

"That's one handsome animal you have there, Mary Elena. He sure is a big boy," a man said.

One woman even asked her if I was for sale! Thank God Mary Elena said no.

When I awoke the next day it was raining hard. The sound of water hitting the metal roof was loud, but soothing.

Mary Elena walked in my stall. *"Neither rain nor snow, will stop us, my friend-we must go now!"* She groomed and dressed me in the appropriate attire and off we went.

My owner discovered I was not fond of the rain. When droplets hit my face I lowered my head and shook them off. She found this to be amusing and laughed.

Even though I didn't want to, I kept riding because the other horses didn't mind getting wet and I didn't want to look like a wuss!

"I see you don't like the rain, Gunner. I wonder how you got through it when you were made to pull a buggy in the rain? I know the Amish wouldn't stop, thus you would have to continue, even if you didn't want to," she said.

Boy, was she right on! My Amish family had made me ride in the pouring rain, lightning, and thunder until we reached our destination.

The dirt roads were mushy and deep, but I had to keep going! I struggled at times to get my footing, but knew if I stumbled or slowed down I would be beat.

But that was then, and this is now! I was no longer with the Amish but with a wonderful gal who treated me well. The least I could do was try my best to make her proud!

───

When we finished training, she took me back to the stable. Because I was so tall I hesitated walking in the stall for it was not as high as Mary Elena's barn.

Sensing my fear she wrapped a towel around the wooden board on top so I wouldn't hit my head going in and out.

Mary Elena also taught me how to "duck" on command to avoid this problem. Boy, was she a good teacher! She should have gotten "Teacher of the Year", for imagine, teaching a big klutz like me to duck my head walking in a stall! Ingenious!

The first week in training my partner was an ex-race horse–a Standardbred gelding from Saratoga Racetrack.

His race name was *'Most Fun Yet,'* but they called him Apollo!

Well, I can tell you he was named wrong, for he wasn't fun at all!

Apollo was fresh off the track, thus a bit sour. He tried kicking me and wasn't pleasant to work with, but people praised us at what a handsome pair we made. When he left the end of the week I had actually grown to like him and sad to see him leave.

Being an ex-racehorse myself, I know how one can get grumpy and sour.

We have to race in all kinds of weather conditions, if we're hurting or sick, or just having a bad day.

The second week Mary Elena's friend, Kim, brought her horse, Storm, to be my new partner.

Storm was a beautiful but sassy rescue. I think she acted that way because she was a bit small and tried intimidating other horses into thinking she was tough. (Like my friend Napoleon)

Right from the beginning Storm and I hit it off.

I really liked her and she liked me. Not the way I liked Maddy of course. I liked Storm like a sister.

During breaks she would rest her tiny head against my neck and fall asleep. I guess she felt safe with me–like I was her big protective brother.

But being a filly, of course Storm had her off-days. One day she was irritable and kicked at another horse. She missed him and hit Mary Elena's brass stirrup, causing a loud noise. We were all startled for this was unlike the quiet, sweet Storm.

Perhaps that is why she was named Storm? You know, 'The calm before the storm,' for you never knew when a period of inactivity would occur and something chaotic would happen. Or perhaps it was just because she was a mare and you know how temperamental they can be!

Horses are classified in four basic personality types. They are:

1. The social horse
2. The fearful horse
3. The aloof horse
4. The challenging horse.

The social horse is quite interactive. He is interested in the world around him. Social horses are the official greeters of the horse world and will most likely welcome you into their personal space. They may struggle with their attention spans when young, just because the world is so interesting to them.

The fearful horse is much more guarded and cautious than his social counterpart, especially when young. He often needs more personal space and may become claustrophobic or panicky when confined. He is more "flight" then "fight" oriented and usually gets all or most of his confidence from a person or another horse.

The aloof horse is not particularly interactive. He is content to be in his own little world and often seems independent of both people and horses. He may have delayed or dull reaction to stimulus or aids and is usually more tolerant than welcoming into his own personal space.

And last but not least is the challenging horse. He has a strong sense of self and may seem prideful or arrogant, especially when young or still entire. A challenging type is usually near the top of the pecking herd and will bully if given the chance.

Horses are just like people who are classified as Type A and Type B personality types. Type A's are organized, ambitious and competitive, while Type B's are more relaxed, less neurotic and frantic.

The next two weeks flew by. The training was hard, but thankfully all 25 students survived and passed.

As Mary Elena loaded me on the trailer she said, *"I am so proud of you Gunner. I know it was tough, especially letting me get on your back, but you did!*

You were brave, reliable, and tried your hardest to learn everything. The other horses were seasoned police horses that have been doing this for years, but it was new to you, my friend!

Now, it's time to go home and see your friends," Mary Elena said.

What! You mean the other horses had already done these things? No wonder it seemed easy to them.

Chapter Twenty-Six

GRADUATION DAY

No Hour Of Life Is Wasted That Is Spent In The Saddle

I want you to know attending police school was no piece of cake, but I learned and perfected many things I never ever dreamed I could.

First, there was formation riding. In class we learned how mounted corps was born. From 1650 to World War I, battles were fought in linear formation. This type of fighting technique required disciplined men and horses to move as one.

The job of the rider is to make her horse feel as much at home at the school as possible. If one horse got out of alignment we would have to do it all over again which could be very stressful and nerve wracking!

We were taught so much in those two weeks. Besides formation riding we learned how to deal with fire, smoke bombs, gunshots, fireworks, and water cans.

Some of it was fun–like re-enacting of the Little Bighorn Battle, Custer's Last Ride, Mounted Cavalry Operations, Cowboy Mounted Shooting, and Hacking and Packing.

We demonstrated 'make-believe' situations, such as performing searches for missing children, pulling cars over, and chasing suspects. We learned Cavalry Tactics, Packer and Pack Animal Handling, Weapons Training, Historical Lessons, Horseback Combative and Mounted Military Operations.

It wasn't easy and at times I wanted to quit and pack it in, but that wasn't me. My mama didn't raise a quitter. Everything I did in life, I gave it my all. Whether it was competing in a horse race, pulling a buggy down cobbled roads, or working on a farm, I did my best!

My work here was now completed and it was time to graduate.

I felt great gratification that I attempted something I thought I could never accomplish–and DID!

It proved that anyone (man or animal) could do ANYTHING they wanted to, if they tried. I never ever thought I would let someone on my back–but I did!

I had the best teacher of course. Mary Elena was assertive in a positive and gentle way. She gained my trust–thus, I allowed her to do the almost impossible.

The only thing I didn't like was practicing protests. People would re-enact protesting by waving signs and flags. During these times I hesitated and shied away.

Mary Elena knew it bothered me and took her time, letting me know this was 'make believe' and nobody was going to really get hurt.

I couldn't tell her I acted this way because it brought back bad memories of being chased and struck—something that will never leave my mind.

Of course Mother Nature didn't cooperate on Graduation Day. It rained throughout the entire ceremony–but as they say, "The show must go on!"

Mary Elena dressed me to the nines and if I say so myself–I looked mighty spiffy! I had a sharp saddle pad, new police saddle, and rosettes attached to my bridle that said "New York."

She was proud of me and told me over and over. I never received so many kisses and hugs as I did that day. The stand was packed with overzealous owners, friends, and fans. As I looked into the audience I saw Kay and her children--my friends who took care of me while I was in quarantine.

When our names were called, I trotted proudly up with Mary Elena.

She received her re-certification diploma and I got a badge I proudly wore on my chest.

I did my very best and it paid off. Mary Elena couldn't have been prouder and I knew mama was watching from up above.

I thought this was the last time I'd be engaging in this type of situation for I had merely been filling in for my friend, Xena.

Little did I know my purpose in life would soon be revealed.

PART FOUR

Chapter Twenty-Seven

MY NEW CAREER

We Can Judge The Heart Of A Man By His Treatment Of Animals

When I returned home my three friends were waiting by the gate. Maddy was standing there with that sultry smile which makes me quiver.

"Welcome home, my friend. We've been waiting for you," Kirby said.

"Thanks for stepping in for me, Gunner. I heard you did fabulous, but had no doubt you would. I'm still not myself so there's no way I could have done it. I owe you, buddy!" Xena uttered.

As a 'thank you' present Mary Elena called a masseuse named Denise to work on me. She was an ex-Standardbred trainer who turned professional equine body worker and boy did she ever make me feel good!

Several weeks had gone by since graduation and things returned to the way they were before. My friends and I would bask in the sun or graze in the green fields where there was plenty of clover to enjoy.

Maddy and I had grown extremely close. Although we could only go so far romantically due to the fact I was gelded, we would kiss and lie beside each other.

Being in love is the best feeling in the world–even for us horses!

I had loved and been loved before--but this time was different. It was a love longer than life and stronger than death.

Every night before falling asleep, I'd say my prayers and thank God for saving me from my old life and giving me this new one!

Maddy was spiritual and also a believer. She taught me 'the horses' prayer' which we would say together. It went:

Feed me, give me water and care for me, and when the day's work is done, give me shelter, a clean bed and a wide stall.

Talk to me, your voice often substitutes for the reins for me.

Be good to me and I will serve you cheerfully and love you.

Don't jerk the reins and don't raise the whip.

Don't beat or kick me when I don't understand you, but rather give me time to understand you.

Don't consider it disobedience if I don't follow your commands.

Perhaps there is a problem with my saddle and bridle or hooves.

Check my teeth if I don't eat, maybe I have a toothache. You know how that hurts.

Don't halter me too short and don't dock my tail.

It's my only weapon against flies and mosquitoes.

And at the end, dear master, when I am no longer any use to you don't let me go hungry or freeze and PLEASE don't sell me.

Don't give me a master who slowly tortures me to death and lets me starve, but rather be merciful and take care of me, by letting me run and enjoy a warm pasture.

Let me request this of you and please don't regard this as disrespectful if I ask in the name of HIM who was born in a stable like me.

Amen.

It was a long prayer but I memorized it. I prayed that man would stop torturing and killing my kind.

I knew many of my friends were not as lucky as me and didn't survive the kill pen!

It broke my heart that so many humans treat animals cruelly. They continue to see us as objects and not the loving, loyal creatures we are!

I didn't know how I was going to do it, but I prayed to God for discernment on how to end this horrible situation.

———

Just when I was getting back to my regular routine, Mary Elena brought me in the barn one night.

'Oh no, this is not good,' I thought. The last time she did this I ended up going to remount school.

"Please Gunner. I know this is asking a lot, but your friend Xena is still in pain from the laminitis and unable to work. There is going to be a huge Memorial Day celebration and I need you to fill in for Xena, once more".

"There's a lot of things I will need to teach you, but I have no doubt you will do great!"

Please don't ask me that again! I did it once and that was enough. I did it for you and Xena, but I'd rather stay here with my friends. I mean, I'm not perfectly sound, either—or haven't you noticed?

As if she read my mind she walked over and kissed my nose. She had the gentlest kisses. They were different than Maddy's, for Mary Elena's were soft and not as wet as Maddy's.

Mary Elena knew exactly how to get to me for she had me wrapped around her finger. I would do anything for that girl! I couldn't say no and agreed to give it one last try!

Chapter Twenty-Eight

SCARE TACTICS

A Dog May Be A Man's Best Friend, But The Horse Wrote History

In order to prepare me for my upcoming adventure, Mary Elena took me to a parking lot filled with motorcycles. At first I freaked out for those machines are downright loud, but after a few minutes I got used to them.

As she rode me a CD played bagpipe music and gunshots to get me accustomed to those sounds.

The morning of Memorial Day, Mary Elena adorned me with a beautiful purple trimmed swallow-tail saddle pad and backward boots in the stirrups.

She explained this symbolized the fallen looking at their friends and family as they left the earth on their way to Heaven.

When I was ready we walked a half-mile to the village in the rain. I don't know what it was with Mother Nature, but she liked to test my nerves, for every time there was a big event, she'd send rain.

Mary Elena sensed my concern.

"You know one thing you can't control my friend is the weather. I know you're not crazy about the rain— especially having to perform in it, but there's nothing we can do. I think of it as God cleansing the earth."

Wow! I never thought of it that way and from that day on the rain didn't bother me as much. I mean the way the world had become, God would have to send a LOT of rain to rid all the evil and ugliness that was here! There had been wars, racial problems and the latest pandemic—the Coronavirus!

Just when everything was going great–that damn pandemic hit, killing hundreds of thousands of people around the world!

A global war had started in China and spread like wildfire worldwide. Efforts to prevent the virus spreading included travel restrictions, quarantines, curfews, and cancellations. Horse races were put on hold, as was other sports.

There were nationwide lockdowns in more than 124 countries.

Being a horse, of course I wasn't informed what was happening and continued life as always. I got up in the morning, was fed, and enjoyed the day grazing in the pasture.

One day Mary Elena walked into the field wearing some kind of funny mask. In fact, every worker wore one. At first it freaked me out for her mouth and nose was covered, but beneath the N95 mask I knew it was Mary Elena for I saw her pretty brown eyes.

She explained what was happening so we weren't frightened. She told us she never lost her faith in God and this is how we would all get through this horrific time. Every day she would pray with us and ask God for His protection over the world, His people, and all His creatures.

It took months to get somewhat back to a normal life, but in the end it seemed the pandemic drew mankind closer together and they now appreciated things they had previously taken for granted.

Now when it rains I see it as God cleansing the earth and actually enjoy it. And another good thing about rain is it brings rainbows and

I love rainbows. Every time I see one I look for the bridge where mother and my friends live, but never find it.

Weeks passed by and I learned many new things. It was now time to take part in my first 'real' event- the State Police Memorial Day Ceremony held at a legion of honor.

When we arrived, a lot of people were waiting to honor the fallen. The horses were lined up behind the building in marching formation and waited–in the rain!

As drops of water hit my face, I dropped my head and shook them off. Mary Elena laughed for she was used to my quirky habit, but the horse next to me gave me a strange look.

I ignored him and held my head high, which wasn't hard because I was by far the tallest.

The motorcycles started their engines.... Rmmmmm rmmmmm rmmmmm!

Wow! It was so loud I thought I might go deaf.

I marched behind the cycles and 50 troopers followed behind us.

Next, was the gun salute. People cried as they were filled with emotion.

Again, I shook my head, but never moved my feet!

The ceremony went well. Right before it ended something flew over my head that scared the living daylights out of me.

It was a drone! A dreaded drone!

This was something entirely new to me and I didn't know what it was. At first I thought it was some kind of huge buzzing insect, so

I began dancing in place. Nobody noticed except Mary Elena.

She sensed my agitation and began rubbing my neck, which always calmed me.

The drone had brought back memories when I was working in the field and got bit by a huge wasp! It felt like the time Doc stuck me with the needle to put me to sleep, but it wasn't–it was a big, ugly bug.

My neck immediately swelled, I began having trouble breathing, a large bump developed, and I started running a fever.

Thank God this happened when I was living with the Yoders, for they immediately called a vet to treat me. If it happened when I lived with one of the other families they most likely would have ignored it and I probably wouldn't be here to tell my story today.

When the ceremony was over we went home victorious and even made the front page of the local newspaper! Mary Elena praised me with lots of kisses. I was pretty darn proud of what I'd accomplished but remembered something mama once told me–always be humble.

Chapter Twenty-Nine

LETTING MY HAIR (MANE) DOWN

God Forbid That I Should Go To Any Heaven In Which There Are No Horses

The day after the Memorial Day ceremony I got to enjoy one of Aunt Denise's massages that kept my muscles from getting tight and sore.

After all, I was now using muscles I didn't even know I had. When you jog or pull a cart you use different muscles than when someone rides on your back.

Funny, but I started enjoying our morning rides. I never thought I would like having someone on my back, but I did! This woman taught me patience, trust, and compassion.

Mary Elena would ride me on secluded trails knowing it was good for my body and mind. That was our special "one on one" time I looked forward to. It was so peaceful and quiet–nothing like my previous homes.

We talked about everything. She even talked to me about God. Nobody had ever discussed Him with me, but my mama. Mary Elena told me she saw God in everything around us: the trees, the wind, the colors of the leaves, and the sky. She told me she even saw God in ME!!

To get to the trails we had to go around the farm and hit the road for a stretch, passing tractors. That's when Mary Elena discovered I wasn't fond of hydraulic cylinder Caterpillars.

"What's the matter, boy? What is it about a tractor that frightens you?

Did something happen to you on a farm?"

When I got within so many feet of a tractor, I'd speed up.

While living on the last farm an inexperienced worker was hired to run a tractor. He was going at a high speed–way faster than he should have, when the machine flipped over landing on a young colt and threw the man into the air. Both died instantly.

The colts dam frantically ran in circles, whinnying, trying to get to her son. It was the most horrifying thing I ever saw and still plays out in my mind today.

Our 'therapeutic' rides consisted of trails and ring work. One day Mary Elena even taught me how to play soccer.

"It's important you learn how to play soccer, for the children love it."

I remembered playing with Ruth, but at that time I picked up the Jolly ball in my mouth and tossed it. Now, Mary Elena taught me how to kick the ball.

At first I was nervous, but after several times doing it I got the hang of it.

I would kick the giant ball and Mary Elena would kick it back to me!

Some days I was on the horse treadmill, which helped get me in shape–just as it does humans.

It was so cool for it relaxed and warmed my muscles while checking my heart rate as the floor vibrated.

Then I was put on a cushion-moving belt and walked for 20 minutes–which was equivalent to one hour by hand.

"You are the best student, Gunner. Next week we will be going to Long Island for a very big event! I think you're ready to show your stuff" she said.

That night Maddy and I were lying on the grass looking at the stars. It was a beautiful July evening and we especially enjoyed nighttime for the flies didn't bite and the intense sun was asleep behind the clouds.

Thousands of twinkling stars illuminated the sky. I told Maddy my mama lived up there with my friends over the Rainbow Bridge.

"The Rainbow Bridge? Where is the Rainbow Bridge? It sounds like a beautiful place. Can we go there, Gunner?" Maddy asked.

I explained the Rainbow Bridge is located somewhere in the sky. When it rains sometimes a rainbow appears and the bridge is behind the rainbow. I told her mama came to me one night and told me all about it. She said the Rainbow Bridge is another worldly place, consisting of a green meadow and a multi-colored prismatic bridge where animals go after they die.

"Die! I don't wanna die", Maddy said. *"Not unless you go with me!"*

I told Maddy I wasn't ready, either, but when we do we'll cross the bridge and go to a lush, green meadow filled with sunshine and love. If you were once sick you will be healed and can run and play as you did when you were young and healthy. There will be no more pain and there's unlimited food, water, toys and treats!

"Wow! That sounds like Heaven," Maddy said.

"It is, silly girl! And when you get there you'll wait patiently until your human companion dies and is reunited with you in the meadow. Then you will cross the Rainbow Bridge together," I explained.

"But what if I die first? How can we go together if you're still here?" she asked yawning.

After thinking of how to answer that I looked over at Maddy and saw she was fast asleep with a smile on her face.

Yes, mama. I'll be there soon enough!

Chapter Thirty

LONG ISLAND

Take My Man—But Stay Away From My Horse!

The next week Mary Elena hooked the truck to the trailer and loaded it with equipment. She said we were going to a very important event in Long Island where there would be hundreds of people.

Poor Xena was still in pain due to the Cushings disease—which is similar to human diabetes. After discussing the situation with the vet, Mary Elena decided the best thing to do would be to retire Xena.

I was glad to hear that for I hated seeing my friend suffer and tippy toe around. Her feet were extremely sore and although she never complained, you could see the pain on her face.

"Hey honey, you are now officially retired. You did your job and were great. I'm showing my thanks by letting you live out your life grazing and playing with your friends," Mary Elena told Xena. *"No more work for you."*

But if Xena was retiring, that meant I would have to take her place! I had mixed feelings, for although I enjoyed my new job, I missed Maddy when I was away. I was hoping Mary Elena would bring her along, but she never did.

"I'm so proud of you, Gunner. You are a real hero!" Maddy said as she nuzzled my neck.

"It takes a real man to step up to the plate and learn a completely new career at your age! And getting over your phobia to let Mary Elena ride you--that takes guts!"

After I said goodbye to my friends, I walked on the trailer and off we went. We drove for several hours listening to country music on the radio. All of a sudden it got very bumpy.

I'm not a fan of riding in a trailer to begin with, but when it got bumpy I became nauseated.

Bumpety, bump, bump–and then the truck stopped.

We were on the Long Island Expressway. Hundreds of cars were flying by honking their horns.

Mary Elena got out of the truck and opened my window.

"Gunner. I got a flat tire on the trailer. I'm going to have to change it and it might take a little while. I'm so sorry buddy, but I'll be as quick as I can.

I know it's scary with all these crazy drivers, but you'll be okay, I promise."

After the tire was changed we continued to our destination.

I heard Mary Elena talking to her friend and she didn't sound happy.

"What the heck! How could they forget to tell me this was taking place at an airport?" she said.

I heard airplanes many times before, but these seemed to be flying right over us. A helicopter soared above my head and boy was it loud!

There were so many people here—especially young children. When they saw me, they ran over and wanted to touch me.

"Gunner--It's so good to see you," said a familiar voice.

I looked around and saw my friend Storm playing soccer with several children.

"Come and join us," Storm said.

The kids were betting on who would win–Storm or me. After we played for a few hours, it ended in a tie!

I have to admit I never had so much fun, but my favorite thing was when the children hugged my head! Their gentle touches and kisses melt my heart. And kids have a special smell to them–like the smell of a puppy dog–so innocent and pure!

I just adore children--always did, and always will. I think I inherited that from mama, for she also loved the little ones. She used to tell me children are a blessing and gift from God.

The ride back home went smoothly—thank God. No flat tires and no more bumps.

Back at the farm, Mary Elena thanked me for doing a great job and gave me kisses. Boy, how I love her kisses!

She prepared a delicious dinner of warm bran mash with apples and honey. She was a smart woman for she knew the way to a man's heart is through his stomach!

"You're getting to be a pro, Gunner. Rest up, honey. Next week we're going to a parade!"

Chapter Thirty-One

MY FIRST PARADE

Virtue Shall Be Bound Into The Hair Of Thy Forelock. I Have Given Thee The Power Of Flight Without Wings

After Long Island, I got a week off. I really missed my friends when I was on the road–especially Maddy–so our one-on-one time was just what the doctor ordered.

It was great just being a horse and doing what I was born to do–eat grass, run free, and entertain people. The crowd of spectators who Mary Elena called "my fan club" grew in numbers.

The first day I arrived at the farm there were 15-20 people. Now anywhere from 50-75 people would show up on Sundays to meet "the gentle giant."

Mary Elena said I was becoming quite a celebrity. Can you believe that? Me, Gun-It, the Standardbred racehorse who never really accomplished anything special in his life— a celebrity!

But that didn't thrill me. I mean I enjoyed making people happy, but all I wanted was to bring awareness of cruelty to horses and shut down all kill pens.

But how could I do that? I can't speak English, so I couldn't be a spokesperson or an advocate. Or could I?

———

That week Mary Elena brought me in at night to groom me. I thought my hair would fall off for she brushed and brushed and brushed me until I shone like a six-carat diamond in Cartier's window.

"You look hot! I've never seen you look so handsome, Gunner. I am so lucky to be your girl," Maddy said batting her lashes.

I was happy she felt that way, but lately I wasn't feeling the greatest. I wasn't sure what was wrong because I was eating, resting, and didn't have a temperature.

Although I wasn't myself, I couldn't let Mary Elena down. The parade was a big thing and I had to do my best!

When we arrived at where the parade was to take place, I saw a lot of motorcycles. They didn't bother me because I was used to those noisy vehicles now; but lined up behind them were big red vehicles I never saw before. Mary Elena sensed my concern and walked me over to check them out.

When I got close, I hesitated for it was HUGE! A man in a uniform came over and introduced himself as Chief Martin.

"Wow, what a big handsome horse," he said. Another man dressed in the same outfit came over to pet me. Both men wore thick wool pants, bright red shirts, black boots, and a red hard hat on their heads.

Mary Elena said they were very important people called firemen who helped prevent or put out fires and save people's lives.

"If you ever want to sell this handsome boy, give me a call," the second man said handing Mary Elena a card. *"My little son would love him."*

I guess she felt my anxiety and whispered in my ear, *"Don't' worry, Gunner. You aren't going anywhere! Only time you will leave me is when you cross the Rainbow Bridge and I hope that's not for a longgggggg time."*

"Now it's time to go to work."

The parade was more fun than work. There were a lot of small children and you know how I feel about kids!

One boy in particular named Timmy—an 8-year-old redhead–followed me around all day. He was the cutest darn thing I seen since little Ruth.

His mother dressed him in a Colonial costume: breeches, button-up shirt with a ruffled collar and a coat.

For some reason he was fascinated with me. He followed and stood by Mary Elena and me the entire day. When we were idle, Timmy would stand by my legs and hug them.

"Timmy is in love with your horse. Although he is very big, if you ever decide to sell him, please call us," the boy's mother said. *"I'm not sure of the price, but I'd really like to take him home."*

Jeez! I wish people would stop asking Mary Elena if I was for sale!

When it was time to leave, Timmy followed us to the trailer and waved goodbye as a tear ran down his freckled face.

Mary Elena said the Parade was a huge success and gave me tons of her special kisses. On the ride home I munched my favorite alfalfa hay and slurped down a bucket of apple juice.

Chapter Thirty-Two

INDEPENDENCE DAY

I Smile When I Catch God Watching Me Through The Eyes Of The Horse

The very first time I heard fireworks I was stabled at the racetrack. They always had a fireworks show after the races on the Fourth of July for the crowd to enjoy.

Fireworks! Those loud, whistling explosive pyrotechnic devices that skyrocket into the air in a variety of colors and shapes and then let out a big BANG!

The first time I heard fireworks I thought someone was shooting a gun. I ran around my stall, but obviously didn't get very far. Molly was also scared and stood in the corner shaking.

It wasn't just me, for every horse in the stable was sweating and trembling. Being the caring man he was, Marvin put earplugs and hoods on all his horses until the fireworks ended. It worked for I never heard a thing.

Marvin said fireworks were originally invented in China to scare away evil spirits and bring about luck and happiness!

I believe they would definitely scare away ANY spirit, evil or good, but how in the heck could they bring luck and happiness?

The Independence Day event was held at the illustrious Goshen Historic track. My friend Storm and another horse named Buck were there. Hundreds of people were waiting to watch the matinee horse races scheduled that day.

It was extremely hot so my friends and I looked for shade. Ironically, the best spot was right next to the track.

I was so excited to watch the races for it brought back a lot of memories: both good and bad. I looked to see if I could find any of my old racing friends, but there were none.

Mary Elena noticed my enthusiasm. *"Don't worry Gunner. You don't have to race today. Those days are long gone honey,"* Mary Elena said.

"But I bet you could really give them a run for their money now. This is the best shape you have ever been in."

The event at the track lasted two days. It was fun watching the horse races for once it's in your blood it never leaves.

Did I miss it? A little, I guess. I enjoyed competing and doing something I was bred to do, but I didn't miss racing when my bones and feet ached.

I didn't miss seeing horses get whipped and beat, and I didn't miss being in accidents.

What I missed was Molly, Pretty Woman, and Cleo; but they wouldn't be here because mama said they lived in Heaven.

I never thought about it until now, but that would mean they were dead. I wondered–how, when and where?

I knew Cleo died from a heart attack, but the others? I hope they didn't suffer. And mama--how did she die? Did she have a painful death? I prayed to God she didn't.

On the second day of the event all I did was play with children. Mary Elena braided my mane with red-white-and blue ribbons in honor of the Fourth of July.

As we walked through the crowd people kept asking to take a photo with me. One child gave me a big hug, kissed my head and wouldn't let go of my leg. When his mother picked him up, he screamed!

The alluring smell of grilled chicken, Bavarian pretzels, hot sausage, elephant ears (they're not really ears of elephants of course, but fried dough with sugar), and popcorn made me hungry.

Several bands were playing music and people danced. There were livestock shows, sheaf tossing, and a rodeo. This was by far the most fun I ever had--I only wished Maddy was here with me to enjoy it.

That night I was totally exhausted. I tried to sleep, but due to several horses coughing in the barn, I tossed and turned. Finally, I fell into a deep sleep.

Chapter Thirty-Three

COMMUNITY DAY

Life's Best Gifts Don't Come From The Mall-They Come From The Barn

By the time we got back to the farm, I was feeling pretty lousy. I know I'm not a youngster anymore, but overall I think I'm pretty healthy.

My aches, pains, and arthritis were something I had learned to deal with, but this was completely different. I didn't want to eat and that's not like me for I'll eat anything, anyplace, anywhere. So when I began leaving my feed, Mary Elena knew something was wrong.

She took my fever and it was 100.7, so she assumed I was just having an off day. We have those days, too–just like you.

———

Our next event was Community Day.

Community Day was a day that brought several communities together. A huge screen was up so the children could watch a movie. Ironically, the movie playing was Black Beauty.

I watched it for I never saw it before. I thought Beauty was so handsome, but he lived a hard life like me. I was leery to find out how the movie would end and if it would be a tearjerker. Luckily, it had a happy ending and Beauty lived happily ever after.

When the movie ended, Mary Elena and I took a stroll around the park. Booths were set up displaying jewelry, clothes, and pottery. Vendors sold everything from food and drink, to arts and crafts.

An array of food was available for purchase, including kettle corn, barbecue ribs, cotton candy, steak hoagies, hot dogs and hamburgers.

Usually when I smell food I crave it, but today the smells made me nauseous.

There was a tent set up for face painting. Artists drew designs of *The Bee and Rainbow, Disney's Frozen Elsa, a Bunny Face, Spiders with Webs, and Beautiful Butterflies* on the sweet children's faces. They looked adorable.

A local television crew was talking to people and taking pictures.

One man walked up to Mary Elena and asked if he could take mine. Although I didn't feel the greatest, I stood with my head high and tried to smile, but couldn't.

———

The children hugged my legs and kissed me on the nose. An 8-year-old girl named Ella followed me the entire day. When it was time to go back to the farm I was more than ready.

After Mary Elena put me on the trailer, little Ella climbed on the wheel of the trailer to pet me one last time.

"One more kiss, Gunner. Plllllllease!" she cried.

She reminded me of Ruth for she would have been about that age now.

Although alfalfa was waiting for me in the trailer bin, I didn't take one bite and when Mary Elena offered me a drink of water, I turned my head.

"Hey buddy. What's wrong? I hope you're not getting sick."

Chapter Thirty-Four

A CLOSE CALL

Take Care Of Your Horse And He'll Take Care Of You

When we arrived at the farm Mary Elena immediately took my temperature. I could see by the look on her face it was not good.

My temperature was now 103. I was coughing and it was difficult to breathe.

Mary Elena immediately called Dr. Wes who told her to quarantine me from the other horses. My nose was running and I was shaking all over, so she covered me with my wool blanket.

Although it was mid-July, I was freezing cold.

The next few days my temperature fluctuated from 101 to 103, my cough persisted, and I had no appetite.

Nighttime was the worst, for all I did was shiver. I know Mary Elena was worried for she stayed with me around the clock. She set up a cot by my stall and slept there, but I don't think she got any sleep for every time I coughed she ran in to check me.

After Doc palpated my lungs and abdomen he collected samples of fluid through a bronchoalveolar lavage.

"Your boy is very sick," he told her.

"Oh no! How could he get sick?" After thinking for several minutes she said, *"Oh my gosh! There were some horses coughing at the fair, but Gunner wasn't near them. They were at the other end of the barn,"* she cried.

"It's airborne. Perhaps he is a little run down and his resistance to fight anything is low. Also, his age doesn't help. I'm going to send these samples out overnight to the hospital. Gunner may have to go there, but until then keep him warm and start him on these antibiotics," he said.

After thinking a few minutes, Mary Elena screamed, *"Oh no. Could Gunner have caught the coronavirus?"*

"I don't know what he has yet, but yes horses can get it, but it's not the same strain as the ones humans get. It's called Equine Coronavirus and has been around since 2010. It's completely different than the human strain and can only be spread through fecal-to-oral transmission," he explained.

"Do you think Gunner caught this at the fair? I disinfected the stall before putting him in it. I would just die if he got something from shipping him to different places."

"Don't blame yourself Mary Elena—these things happen. But he must remain quarantined. I'll give you anti-inflammatory meds that will help," said Doc.

When Dr. Wes came back the next day he told Mary Elena he had good and bad news. The good news was I didn't have equine coronavirus but a strain of pneumonia called herpes virus, which was viral.

The bad news is I had a severe case and because of my age it would take longer to cure.

Twice a day my temperature, blood pressure, respiration rate, and pulse was taken and recorded. I began to eat a little, but that was only after Mary Elena fed me warm bran mash.

"Please Gunner, get better honey. I don't know what I'll do if something happens to you. I blame myself for taking you so many places. I didn't know sick horses were there."

I looked in her eyes and batted my lashes letting her know it wasn't her fault at all. I know she understood for she crawled in the stall, curled up beside me, put her head on my neck, and wrapped her arms around me.

She looked up and started to pray.

"Please God, make Gunner well again. He is the best thing that ever happened to me, and I need him," she cried.

That night my fever broke. After Mary Elena left to take a shower I fell into a deep sleep. When I opened my eyes Mama was standing in my stall. I blinked to make sure I wasn't dreaming, but she was as real as could be.

She looked beautiful and smelled like lavender, camphor, and lemon. The smell was very strong.

She looked exactly like she did the last time she came to me in my dreams, but this time she wore no ribbons in her mane.

Mama looked at me with her big brown eyes and started to cry.

"Mama please don't cry. Why are you so sad?" I asked her.

"You're my son and I don't want to see you sick, but God told me not to worry for He is taking care of you. He is so proud of what you're doing, as I am, but He told me you are not done here yet. It won't be long before you can come live with Molly, Pretty Woman, Cleo and me.

Oh, and Cleo says to tell you she's happy you are in love again for you have enough love for both her and Maddy."

Mama started to walk away.

"Mama, please don't leave me again. I need you."

She came closer and kissed my head. I could feel her kiss and smell her sweet breath, so I knew this wasn't a dream.

"Honey, I'll never leave you. I'm always there--right in your heart. Keep looking for the Rainbow Bridge and you will see me there."

I wanted to tell her I always look but never see it, but she was gone.

Chapter Thirty-Five

AN AMERICAN HERO

Learn This Well.... The Last Ride Is Never The Last Ride And The End Is Not The End

After two weeks stall rest, Mary Elena turned me out with my friends. Boy, were they were glad to see me!

"We were worried about you Gunner. We wanted to come and see you but weren't allowed", Kirby said. *"Poor Maddy was worried sick. She paced the fence day and night."*

"I wasn't feeling very good, but I'm better now. And I missed you, too," I said.

———

Back in the farmhouse Mary Elena told her boyfriend, Marc,

"There's a big ceremony next week, but I'm not sure if Gunner is up to it."

"Why not leave it up to Gunner? Ask him if he wants to go. He'll let you know if he's up to it. If not, maybe you can take Maddy," he said.

"Maddy's not quite ready, but I'm not going to make Gunner go if he's not 100%. The poor thing has been through enough, and at his age we have to be extra careful."

Mary Elena came outside and walked up to me.

"Gunner, there's a very big event next week in New York. If you're not up to it, you don't have to go, honey."

I knew what she was asking. Although I really didn't want to there was no way I could turn her down. I put my head on her shoulder, which was my way of telling her I'd go.

"Okay, buddy. Let's get you ready," she said.

That week she bathed, brushed, and trimmed my mane. Each day I was getting stronger and feeling more like myself.

———

At the fair dozens of horses lined up in front of a big stage.

Mary Elena walked me to my designated spot and we waited. Not sure what I was waiting for, but I stood perfectly still.

Just then a helicopter swooped down, landing on a marked area in the grass. A man emerged followed by 2 burly bodyguards. I knew he was someone important for the crowd roared and clapped.

Reporters, television crews and photographers began taking pictures. The man was introduced as the Governor of New York who was there to help celebrate the grand opening.

The Governor walked through the crowd, greeting and shaking peoples hands. He made his way over to the horses and stopped in front of us.

"And what's your horses name?" he asked Mary Elena.

"His name is Gunner, sir," she said.

"What a big handsome horse," he said.

Journalists and photographers began surrounding us. Cameras flashed and microphones held up hoping to get an interview. Everyone wanted to know who I was and my story.

I listened as Mary Elena told them I was a Standardbred she rescued from the kill pen. Hearing her tell my story, I felt sad.

I had pretty much blocked out that part of my life, never wanting to go there again.

It appeared everyone was touched for they all wanted to hug and kiss me. As soon as the Governor got on the copter and it flew away I relaxed. I was glad the event was over and anxious to get back home.

"Gunner, you rocked! I am sooooooo proud of you. It's now time for lunch, and then back to the barn for a little rest before the main event at the coliseum," Mary Elena said with a smile.

"What! You mean it's not over?" I grumbled.

Chapter Thirty-Six

THE COUNTY FAIR

The Horse Is A Mirror To Your Soul...
And Sometimes You Might Not Like
What You See In The Mirror

Early that evening we arrived at the coliseum. Hundreds of children were waiting to see the horses. When they saw me, once again I was the crowd favorite because of my size.

I soon discovered the event was far from over. In fact, I heard Mary Elena talking to another woman saying we would be there another two weeks!

I was disappointed for I wanted to go home and see my girl.

Horses are like dogs–they really don't have a perception of time–they are creatures of habit. They seem to know exactly when it is time for their breakfast, lunch, or dinner. They will wait by the stall door and bang their bucket or paw in anticipation.

But as far as knowing if it is one, two, or three days–it is unknown.

Every morning I attended the horse education seminar held in a tent with various breeds of horses. One was selected to represent their breed. There was a Thoroughbred, Percheron, Clydesdale, Paint, and myself representing the Standardbred.

The children wanted to know everything about me and Mary Elena did a wonderful job telling them. As I listened my heart ached hearing how I had been mistreated, for like I said, I managed to bury those memories in the back of my mind. Children were crying as they heard my tale. Even the adults shed tears.

Mary Elena explained how she rehabilitated me, and the journey to get where I was today. I noticed one journalist in particular really seemed interested. After the session she introduced herself to Mary Elena.

"Hello. My name is Kristina Lowe and I work for CKA television. I am taken with your horse's story and would like to get more information from you, if possible. Could we meet somewhere so we can talk further?"

Mary Elena was stunned, but answered, *"Of course. Here's my number. Perhaps you can visit the farm one day."*

We remained at the fair for two weeks. Every day I was assigned a new job, such as playing with children, leading other horses in a parade, and standing guard making sure things were in order.

I was back to my old self again. I never rode more than I did those two weeks. Mary Elena took me from one end of the fair to the other. We would pass the farm animals, vendors selling crafts, people dressed in costumes and a damn train that buzzed by every day at noon.

I'm not fond of trains for they go too quick and toot that horn that scares the daylights out of me every time I hear it.

Each morning we walked by the antique tractor display. No, we didn't walk–I rushed passed it for it brought back bad memories I had encountered on the Amish farms.

In the evening the horses participated in the parade. It was dark as we passed the Ferris wheel and rolling coaster. The screaming of the kids spooked the other horses, but when they saw I was okay with it, they calmed down. Mary Elena said I was a brave boy and a good role model others looked up to.

It was time for the opening ceremony and they were looking for someone to carry the flag. I heard Mary Elena volunteer and prayed they didn't. Unfortunately, they did, and we were chosen!

She was handed and held the flag as we squeezed into the narrow entry, leading a dozen horses into the coliseum. Cameras flashed and people clapped and cheered.

Finally, the fair was over and it was time to go home. Hallelujah!

"Thank you so much, my friend. You were great once again. I can never repay you for stepping up and doing something you never thought you could," Mary Elena whispered. *"Gunner is a rock star!"*

Chapter Thirty-Seven

AN UNEXPECTED INJURY

I Can Make A General In Five Minutes, But A Good Horse Is Hard To Replace
Abraham Lincoln

Several weeks after the State Fair my friends and I were turned out in the large field on the farm. It was a cold, windy day as fall approached. I always preferred cold to hot weather for it made me feel frisky like I was a youngster again.

We chased one another, bucking and kicking. As I ran down hill I stepped in a deep hole made by a groundhog. An excruciating pain shot up my leg. I stopped in my tracks and started limping.

Kirby came over, *"Gunner. Hey buddy, what happened?"*

"I stepped in a hole and my leg hurts like hell!" I said.

Mary Elena saw me and ran over.

"Oh no. Gunner, what happened?"

After checking my leg, she brought me in the barn and called the vet.

I knew it was serious for I had never felt so much pain, even with my racetrack injuries.

After Dr. Wes examined me he said, *"Looks like Gunner did a good job pulling his check ligament. I'd say he'll be off a good six months."*

What did you say, Doc? Six months! No way! I have a job here and it's not done yet. Mary Elena, I'm so sorry I let you down.

For the next eight months Mary Elena cared for me as if I were an entry in the Kentucky Derby. I still didn't know why she took such good care of me, for I was just an average horse.

I never accomplished anything in my eighteen-years to write home about, so why did she put her time and hard earned money into me?

Every day she iced and poulticed my leg. Although I missed being in the field with my friends, I was beginning to enjoy this easy life.

It seems when you have down time, whether from an injury or sickness, you think a lot. I thought about how my life was–from the racetrack, to becoming an Amish horse–ending in a kill pen.

People surmise that horses can't think and remember. Well, that's not true for I remembered everything. Mama and how she loved and cared for me. Bill and Karen, my first 2-legged parents. Marvin and Cathy and little Stan. Hannah, Jacob, and the children—especially little Ruth. The two Amish families who were cruel to me. Pretty Woman, Cleo, and Molly. And now living here with Mary Elena, Maddy, Xena and Kirby.

God has certainly blessed me. Even through the bad times He watched over me. Mama always said 'things happen for a reason,' and I guess she was right.

My journey has not always been easy and pleasant, but look where I am today! It took pain and abuse to make me appreciate what I have now.

During my convalescence Mary Elena began teaching Maddy how to become a police horse. I watched them from my stall and was so proud of my girl. Maddy sure was a beauty.

———

That winter had been brutal, and I was glad to see it end. The robins began singing their songs and flowers bloomed. My leg healed great, thanks to my nurse and I was anxious to get back on the road and resume my duties.

"Gunner, I've been schooling Maddy and I think she's almost ready, but she still is afraid of being next to a horse. Ever since a horse kicked her she is scared of it happening again. I know she trusts you, so please help build her confidence."

The next several weeks Maddy and I worked side-by-side, helping her overcome her fear and learning to trust again.

I loved teaching her things and she learned the ins and outs quickly. Not only was my girl beautiful–she was smart!

Chapter Thirty-Eight

DREAMS CAN COME TRUE

What The Colt Learns In Youth, He Continues In Old Age

Mark Twain once said, *"The two most important days in life are the day you are born and the day you find out why."*

I certainly was lucky the day I was born for God gave me the best mother in the world. Even today I am still not sure what my purpose in life is but I believe it has something to do with helping save my fellow horses from the kill pen.

After my leg healed Mary Elena took Maddy along with us to a special event held at the Goshen Historic Track. It was great having Maddy on the road with me. At first my girl was a little leery of getting kicked by another, but I gave her the confidence and assurance she needed. After all, I was there with her and I wouldn't let ANYthing happen to my Maddy.

I thought Mary Elena couldn't have picked a better spot for Maddy's debut for the Goshen Historic Track is a quaint and beautiful place and the oldest harness racing track in history. The Harness Racing Hall of Fame is there and if you've never seen it, make sure you do. Since I had been there before, I knew my way around.

In 2017 a devastating fire destroyed a barn at the Goshen track but had recently been renovated.

Scheduled that day were 9 live races. Legendary race announcer Roger Huston was there to call the races and top drivers were listed to drive the horses.

The Governor was scheduled to fly in on his helicopter for a ribbon cutting ceremony, but it was pretty hush-hush what it was for.

At first the clouds were threatening but soon gave way to an intense bright sun. Being it was July the humidity was high, the temperature was in the 80's, and there was only a 0 per cent chance of rain.

The magnificent Clydesdales paraded onto the track in front of a packed audience. The grandstand was filled with people from all walks of life.

The iconic team of horses pulled their legendary red wagon and harness drivers posed for pictures with eager fans in the Winners Circle.

One of the Clydesdale's kept flirting with Maddy. It really ticked me off and I gave him a dirty look. She knew it bothered me and being the sweetheart she is, ignored him.

There were so many things to do at the fair. A concert was scheduled that evening with my favorite country star–Billy Currington, and a wedding was to take place in the winner's circle after the races.

There were games, arts and crafts, face painting, car shows, fun runs, and food, food, food–something for everyone.

The children loved petting Maddy and me. At first they were intimidated by our size but when they saw we were gentle, they hugged and kissed us.

When Race 1 was called out to the track, I started to sweat. Mary Elena noticed and asked me what was wrong. I began pacing back and forth, which started to make Maddy uneasy.

"Gunner. What's wrong? Do these races upset you?" Mary Elena asked.

The races didn't bother me. I just didn't like hearing the horses get whipped, and if the horses didn't race well, they might end up in the kill pen, like I did.

Sensing my anxiety, Mary Elena brought Maddy and me back to the barn and fed us. When we were finished eating she brushed us and braided our manes with red, white, and blue ribbons.

It was now time for the ribbon cutting ceremony. Mary Elena rode me, and her friend, Kim, rode Maddy. We went to our designated spots near the grandstand with the other horses.

The helicopter carrying the Governor descended landing in a roped off area.

Maddy began fussing as the copter came down, but I assured her everything was okay.

When the governor walked on stage he looked through the crowd, as if he was looking for someone in particular. He spotted Mary Elena and motioned her to the grandstand.

She was startled, but rode me up.

"Before we start the ribbon cutting ceremony, I want to take time to honor a very courageous and noble American hero. After a turbulent life as a race and Amish horse he was discarded like a piece of trash and sent to a kill pen. Thankfully, a compassionate woman rescued and rehabilitated him.

The horse I am talking about is the spokes horse for all equines, who when their racing career is over and are no longer wanted, they are shipped to a kill pen and sold for meat price. Something has got to be done to end this inhumane situation and he will be the one to make it happen! I'm talking about an eighteen-year-old Standardbred horse named Gun It. I officially name today "Gunner Day", he said.

The look on Mary Elena's face was priceless. Speechless she smiled from ear to ear.

I wasn't sure if I heard him right, but I must have for Maddy was beaming and the crowd clapped and cried.

Just then it began to rain lightly. There was zero chance of rain in the forecast and the skies were bright blue–but a raincloud appeared directly over Mary Elena and me–-and just for a minute it rained.

It lasted but a minute then stopped. Just then a beautiful rainbow appeared in the sky. It was the most beautiful rainbow I'd ever seen for the colors were brighter than usual. Everyone looked at it in awe.

I stared at the sky and squinted from the sun. In the middle of the rainbow was a small bridge. I wasn't sure if anyone else saw it, but I sure did.

And then I saw my mother! It was as clear as if she was standing right in front of me.

She smiled as a tear ran down her face. The tear fell from the sky and landed on my nose.

Standing next to her was Pretty Woman, Cleo and Molly! They were all smiling.

I was distracted for a minute when the Governor said, *"I am officially naming today 'Gunner Day' and giving him the key to the city."*

He handed Mary Elena a key. She threw her arms around my neck and kissed me.

I looked at the sky but the bridge and mama were gone!

Chapter Thirty-Nine

THE END OF A BEAUTIFUL STORY

The Wind Of Heaven Is That Which Blows Between A Horse's Ears

After the fair my life changed dramatically. I really didn't understand what it meant having a day named after me or getting a key to the city.

I didn't know where the door was located that the key would open, but I'm sure Mary Elena did.

We made the front page of the New York Times and were 'the buzz' on several local shows where I was being called a hero–but I didn't feel like one.

Mary Elena was proud of me, as was Maddy, Kirby, and Xena. But what really mattered was that my mama saw the ceremony.

I know there's still a lot of work to be done to bring awareness to the horrible situation happening to many horses and I will work until the day I die trying to end it.

I don't go to many events with Mary Elena anymore, for she now takes Maddy most of the time– who is doing a fabulous job. I'm so thankful for my arthritis has been really getting the best of me lately.

I have a new job and purpose. I spend most of my time on the farm teaching young junior police horses and riders formation riding. Once a week school children come to visit and I cherish those days.

I still have my own massage therapist, body worker, acupuncturist, and nutritionist who make sure I'm healthy and safe.

Maddy and I are more in love than ever. Of course we can't get married and have babies, but we're okay with that as long as we're together.

Mary Elena is planning on building a rescue facility solely for rehab and police horse training and I have no doubt she will get it done. She is truly an angel in blue jeans and I am so blessed to spend my remaining days on earth with her.

Every night I thank God for all He has done for me.

Whenever it rains I look for the Rainbow Bridge in the sky. I never did see mama again after that day, but that's okay. She knows what I'm doing and when it's my time to go home, I'll proudly trot across the Rainbow Bridge knowing I fulfilled my purpose on earth!

THE END

To Be Continued

Epilogue

Imagine a world where horses took their bad owners to the auction!

In the real world, it's just the opposite. Not necessarily bad horses, for there is no such thing.

A horse is a gentle, loving, and loyal creature. Unfortunately, many humans are not.

The horse is one of God's favorite creations. In His omniscience God created the horse for man. He gave it great strength to carry us through life. He gave it great beauty that we would be astounded whenever He chased the wind, and He gave it great heart because we needed to see courage. Most of all, He gave it the capacity to trust, so that we might earn it.

Horses are one of four most commonly abused animals in the United States; joining cats, dogs, and livestock. Once a horse is abused he will always be on guard to defend himself.

When an abused mare has a foal she teaches her baby to react the way she would in the face of danger. Thus, the pattern begins.

The story of Gunner is true and many horses sadly live a life like his, but don't have a happy ending. Statistically, 100,000 horses are sent to slaughter every year in the United States alone.

Slaughter is a brutal and terrifying end for horses and is inhumane. On the way to horse death row they are shipped for more than 24 hours at a time without food, water, or rest in crowded trucks.

No horse deserves to be in a kill pen or to suffer the horrific journey to slaughter.

Gunner is one of the lucky ones given a second chance in life. Hopefully his story will bring much needed awareness and closure to this horrific situation.

About the Author

Victoria Howard is an internationally published author and an avid horse lover who has bred, owned, raised, and raced Standardbred horses for 40 years.

She has appeared on Fox & Friends, Good Day Sacramento, Good Morning Kentucky, and Good Day L.A. with several of her books. Her work has been highlighted in The New York Times, The Pittsburgh Press and The Huffington Post.

Victoria holds several beauty titles and once represented her state in the Mrs. USA Pageant in Las Vegas.

In 2011 she was voted "Woman of the Year" by Who's Who Worldwide.

Victoria lives in Florida with her family.

The Rainbow Bridge

Just this side of Heaven is a place called Rainbow Bridge.

When an animal dies that has been especially close to someone here, that pet goes to Rainbow Bridge.

There are meadows and hills for all our special friends so they can run and play together.

There is plenty of food, water and sunshine, and our friends are warm and comfortable.

All the animals who had been ill and old are restored to health and vigor; those who were hurt or maimed are made whole and strong again, just as we remember them in our dreams of days and times gone by.

The animals are happy and content, except for one small thing; they each miss someone very special to them, who had to be left behind.

They all run and play together, but the day comes when one suddenly stops and looks into the distance. His bright eyes are intent; his eager body quivers. Suddenly he begins to run from the group, flying over the green grass, his legs carrying him faster and faster.

You have been spotted, and when you and your special friend finally meet, you cling together in joyous reunion, never to be parted again. The happy kisses rain upon your face; your hands again caress the beloved head, and you look once more into the trusting eyes of your pet, so long gone from your life, but never absent from your heart.

Then you cross Rainbow Bridge together.

*In Memory Of All The Horses We Have Loved and Lost

Other Equine Books Written by Victoria M. Howard

Meadow Skipper (Co-wrote with Bob Marks)

Junior: The Horse That Won The Kentucky Derby

Roosevelt Raceway: Where It All Began (Co-wrote with Billy Haughton & Fred Hudson)

Junior and Elena: A Horse Love Story

The Adventures of Max and Molly

Murray Brown (Co-wrote with Bob Marks)

The Voice: The Life of Roger Huston

Kentucky Horse Park: Paradise Found

Printed in the United States
By Bookmasters

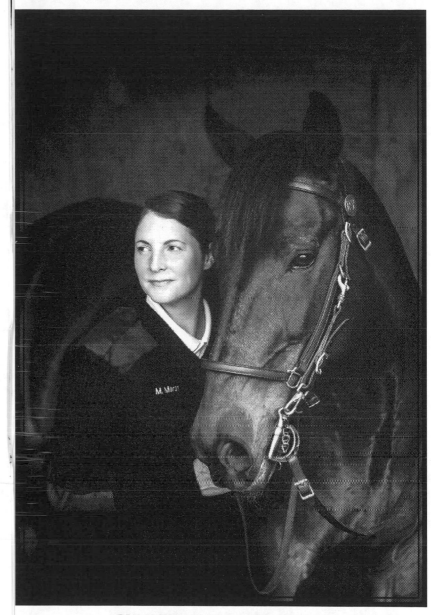

GUNNER AND MARY ELENA